Giuseppe Bono

BLUE PAPERS

Studies on digitational architecture

APPLIED
RESEARCH
+DESIGN
PUBLISHING

APPLIED
RESEARCH
+DESIGN
PUBLISHING

Published by Applied Research and Design Publishing, an imprint of ORO Editions.
Gordon Goff: Publisher

www.appliedresearchanddesign.com
info@appliedresearchanddesign.com

USA, EUROPE, ASIA, MIDDLE EAST, SOUTH AMERICA

Author: *Giuseppe Bono*
Preface: *Pilar Maria Guerrieri*
Book Design: *Domenica Bona*
Project Manager: *Alejandro Guzman-Avila*
Managing Editor: *Jake Anderson*

10 9 8 7 6 5 4 3 2 1 First Edition

Library of Congress data available upon request. World Rights: Available

ISBN: 978-1-951541-91-0

Color Separations and Printing: ORO Group Ltd.
Printed in China.
International Distribution: www.appliedresearchanddesign.com/distribution

ORO Editions makes a continuous effort to minimize the overall carbon footprint of its publications. As part of this goal, ORO Editions, in association with Global ReLeaf, arranges to plant trees to replace those used in the manufacturing of the paper produced for its books. Global ReLeaf is an international campaign run by American Forests, one of the world's oldest nonprofit conservation organizations. Global ReLeaf is American Forests' education and action program that helps individuals, organizations, agencies, and corporations improve the local and global environment by planting and caring for trees.

Preface

by Pilar Maria Guerrieri

Let me begin by saying, without anticipating to the readers what Giuseppe Bono's *Blue Papers* has to say, there is no doubt that this is an interesting book. With its innovative approaches and comprehensive referencing, it analyses the contemporary digital shift and its implications within the architectural realm.

After years of practising architecture in several countries around the world, an incredible passion for research, and ongoing studies in robotics and architectural computation conducted inside the B-Pro MSc Architectural Computation at The Bartlett School of Architecture (UCL), have made it possible for Bono to construct a satisfying and original picture of the impact that digital technologies have in architectural design and inside the construction industry. Such digital impact analysed from different perspectives, from practice to education, provides a 360-degree study of particular relevance.

However, it is not only in this perspective that the study is interesting. *Blue Papers* contributes a significant degree to the debate around the relationship between the human being and the computational machine. It is currently evident that such relationship cannot be avoided, and new research is imperative to capture its perspective. As Bono states, the current digital turn in architecture "is a matter of human progress rather than a mere technological development".

The book has been written at a particularly complex and contradictory time in the contemporary world, a time where multidisciplinary approaches have become more and more mandatory. Bono's book has been trying to analyse the current digital evolution of architecture, keeping the balance between written papers and experimental projects, a decision that well reflects Bono's background as an architect. The visual apparatus is very explanatory of the imaginative digital potential. It is clear from the beginning that the book is written by an architect and not by a historian in the way it explains from within crucial topics and tools related to architectural digitisation. It demonstrates a deep knowledge of the ongoing technological innovation, such as computational design and robotics, being able to showcase its potentials to the readers and, at the same time, becoming a tool for practitioners.

A virtue of the book is that it reads the digital shift in a proactive way, always keeping a balance between technology and humanities. In fact, often, one sees that technologists are in love with technology in itself and far from real challenges, whereas humanists address technology without really knowing the new tools and their potentials. This book does have the merit to attempt creating a bridge between the two realities. Bono has a hybrid educational and professional profile that allows him to address the current digital turn in architecture towards a technological and at the same time humanistic perspective.

However, acknowledging the incredible potential of the digital realm, I would like to point out certain critical considerations that came to my mind while reading the book and which might be an inspiration for further observations.

Anonymity vs authorship

Bono recognises the great potential of the digital revolution and its large impact, mainly on Western society. He defines it as a 360-degree cultural shift and not just a simple technological innovation. A shift that also implied a radical change in the figure of the architect, who—in Bono's terms—is increasingly becoming a *digitational architect*. An architect who not only knows how to use technological tools but also how to address them inside of a wider context of reference; beyond the mere technological development and towards a panoptic understanding of a new human progress. The presence of computational tools and methods, increasingly predominant in design and construction, raises a question that is not secondary with respect to the authorship of projects: the more the machine becomes responsible for the result of the architectural project, both structural and aesthetic, the more it will necessarily tend to standardise, compared to the much more intuitive and unpredictable human creativity; no matter how much it may be possible to customise the final result modifying the inputs given. A process that optimises, but also ultimately impoverishes the final project.

The appeal is to find ways to maintain control of the final architectural output and not let concerns of greater efficiency and economy reducing architecture to data input, leaving to an algorithmic jungle the wonderful world of design, and projecting us into even more repetitive architectural scenarios than those that already characterise the world we are living in.

The interpretation factor

The digital revolution, as Bono clearly shows us, has in most cases led to optimisation processes, but this efficiency is not necessarily the most important goal to be achieved. Solving the great contemporary challenges, or at least trying to do so, is the goal. It is not always understood by technocrats that the digital revolution, the technological innovation, and the development of its tools are always medium—never the final goal.

The old-fashioned architecture, if we can define it that way, being intermediated much less by cold numbers and data, gave ample space and margins to emotional and critical interpretation, with all its approximations. Interpretation, often slow and tentative of places, context, atmospheres, psychological aspects, and cultural nuances of various kinds were the projects' soul. Interpreting situations in an emotional way is something that machines are not able to do yet. Computational machines can respond to pre-set parameters, calculate, and create projections based on data but cannot design emotionally, imagine, project freely. The ability to interpret is key in reading situations and finding key issues to solve, understanding which ones give real priority. It is a visionary ability. In fact, something that may appear irrelevant from the numbers could, instead, be something with a great implicit potential to develop. Machines do not have visions; they execute according to commands. Digital technology has, in fact, a terrible tendency to eradicate the complexity of natural issues, providing efficient solutions—devoid of critical and emotional interpretations—that often create more hypothetical questions than real answers.

Information overload

Bono highlights the power of *connectocracy*, namely the power of connections that the digital age has made available to us. By doing so, he also shows the implicit speed at which these connections are possible today. Connections at all levels have substantially changed the way we conceive design as a whole. Easy accessibility has changed models, often leading to more amateurism in research and a profound change in aspirations. At the digital level, where everything is accessible and therefore seems feasible, solutions are imagined for one place due to free and fluid information but may be inspired by another place. Perhaps the inspiration is taken online from a very different place in climate, culture, and materials; not taking into account the diversity of contexts.

The access to new reference parameters has determined a good dose of superficiality and has created certainties instead of doubts, adjustments, and adaptations. Even if the design was slower in the past, slowness was sometimes a value: it dismissed, chose, adjusted, and finally—as a result of this long process—crafted the final design.

The middleman

I agree with what Bono says about the great digital potential, the new opportunities that the digital world opens up for the built environment and its efficiency. Digitisation is an innovation process that it is impossible to avoid. However, I believe though that there is a subtle implication involved by digital technologies that has not been considered enough: the constant need for the presence of a tech expert, a middleman between the design and its realisation. Unfortunately, digital technologies, programmes, and artificial machines are not intuitive yet. They need a professional capable of dealing with their complexity during the design process. This high level of technology needs the constant presence of someone capable of sorting out tech-related issues; allowing the machines and programmes work, understand, and write in computer language. Being able to translate that computer language into reality, communicating the digital inputs to physical workers. Such skills create an inevitable gap between the machine and those who build. It is very important to work on the accessibility and simplicity of use of these digital tools by everyone, avoiding the mandatory presence of a middleman.

Disparity

Bono highlights scenarios of new possible teaching methods through new forms of multidisciplinarity. His vision can certainly be shared, although we must not forget the disparity of possibilities that different contexts present. Digital technologies and its new potential are still very costly, buying a computer is expensive, new software, time and investment to keep up with updates involve constant costs, and not everyone can afford it. We must be aware that the potential of the digital revolution, in the way the author presents it, is not yet ready to face less developed realities, such as those of the poorest countries or the most marginalised rural areas in most parts of the world. So it is true that this is an extraordinary possibility but, as of today, it runs the risk of creating bigger disparities at social level, between those who are rich and those who are poor, between those who are educated and those who are not, between those who can afford the digital innovation and those who cannot. This is an issue that cannot be addressed ex-post because, at that point, it will be too late. The digital world must defend the values of democracy and try to orientate itself from the beginning towards the most difficult and less fortunate realities, always offering an opportunity to contain the social gap and not be the cause of it. The digital innovation yes, but at what price?

As Mies van der Rohe taught us: "The new era is a fact: it exists, irrespective of our yes or no. Yes, it is neither better nor worse than any other era. It is a pure datum, in itself without value content". Digitisation is a fact; it is not just a matter of concern of architects but a global evolution that we face every day. Acknowledging it is fundamental to face contemporary challenges, we should make the most of it, but never losing our critical perspective. By staking out a position on the field, Bono establishes himself with prospective readers as a reliable reference to future digital development in the architectural realm. The book is an eyeopener and a very valid starting point for future research.

Index

Introduction | Nonconclusion

Introduction: A step to make

During the last thirty years, the use of digital technologies in architecture has exponentially increased. New computational tools and methods are significantly changing the way we design and perform our buildings. In addition to that, the advancement in the field of digital fabrication and robotics is giving life to new automated systems able to promote new integrative and co-evolutionary approaches which are moving the construction industry towards more efficient and sustainable processes. Although the integration of computation and robotics in architectural design and construction is becoming a central aspect in contemporary architectural practice, the definition of "digital architecture" coming from such technological advancement is still very problematic. In this regard, there are two main criticalities related to the application of the word "digital" inside an architectural context: the problem of style and the problem of materiality. From one side, since being digital involves the process of digitisation—namely the conversion of physical matter into virtual formats—the "digital" itself cannot be responsible for any architectural style since it cannot force a designer to operate according to verifiable forms. On the other hand, architecture as a social construction implies the consolidation of urban realities inside an analogue world, and by definition, "analogue" is opposite to "digital": the digital form is immaterial, while architecture refers to material buildings. It is appropriate to say that the digital design of buildings may exist but only in the realm of immaterial models since building themselves can only be analogue. Whether it is accepted or not, architecture is real; it physically forms the built environment which shapes our life; it represents a point of view and a decision, namely what we decide to pass on to future generations.

The observations highlighted so far validate the fact that the contemporary formulation of "digital architecture" is reaching an impasse. For someone, digital architecture is a sum of technological tools; for others, a system of advanced methods. In both cases, the understanding of digital architecture has historic paradigm shift is still far from its completion, and such a delay of understanding represents a significant part of the

confusing and slippery territory in which architecture is currently developed. The reasons for such delay lie in a multitude of paradoxes affecting
the current digital society; more likely, such uncertainty might be generated by the fact that both tools and methods are not enough to understand the measure of a new paradigm. Understanding the real measure of
digital architecture—in other words, understanding it as a new paradigm
shift—means rectifying the need to consider digital architecture as a matter of human progress rather than a mere technological development: this
is the step to make.

In a context of significant debate and reappraisal of the architectural discipline, the current book *Blue Papers. Studies on Digitational Architecture*
collects a series of theoretical writings and projects moving towards a different understanding of the current digital development in architecture,
namely considering it as a matter of human progress rather than mere
technological development. In order to understand the title of the publication, an explanation is required about the meaning of the word *digitational*. The word *digitational* is generated by the combination of the word
"digital" and the word "computational", two complementary but different terms inside the formulation of a contemporary operative architecture: the former considered as a matter of human progress, while the latter
as a matter of technological development. Such complementary division
is based on the distinction between the words "progress" and "development", with the former representing an ideal concept while the latter a
pragmatic and economic notion. For this reason, replacing the word "digital" with the word *digitational* reflects the intention to emphasise the
paratactic relationship between technology and humanity inside the current digital society, two faces of equal importance belonging to the same
coin. Similarly, using the word *digitational* in an architectural context means considering contemporary architecture as a constant interaction between technological tools and human input, namely the balance between
human intelligence and artificial intelligence.

Applying the word *digitational* to architecture requires the answer to an initial question: what is *digitational architecture*? Referring to the previous
explanation of such word, *digitational architecture* is the architecture in
the age of digitisation and computation. It combines the human progress
promoted by digitisation—namely the tendency of converting everything
related to the physical world into new virtual formats—and the technological development generated by computation—namely the action of producing answers through mathematical calculations and the use of machines. Prefiguring an operative architecture in the middle of digitation and
computation requires an appropriate vocabulary made by a new language
and new words. In a time where a bulimic evolution of language is continuously generating new words able to feed a constant concentration and

reduction of meanings, what is the need for defining a further term? In other words, what is the reason behind the definition of a *digitational architecture*?

As already highlighted above, having a closer look at the ongoing architectural debate—and perhaps moving the starting point a couple of decades further back—it is possible to see that the formulation of digital architecture is reaching a critical point. In fact, after around thirty years spent in expanding the architectural discipline towards new digital methods of design and fabrication, we are still arguing if digital architecture may exist or not. The definition of *digitational architecture* extends the current notion of digital architecture towards a different understanding of its principles, namely considering contemporary architecture as sedimentation of technological development inside a background of human progress, a point of pertinent crisis to be intended as a sum between evaluation, judgment and decision. At the current state of our time, digital architecture is still a matter of avant-garde, a symptom of the transaction from ordinary to extraordinary research. In such a background of ongoing experimentation, digital architecture might exist, but only if we consider it as the virtual avatar of a real identity. The reality of such identity crosses the impossible architectural condition of being digital, and the definition of a *digitational architecture* responds to the intention to overcome such impossibility. *Digitaltional architecture* combines the socio-political and anthropological implication of being digital with the use of computational tools and methods: in other words, *digitational architecture* is the combination of digital humanities and computational technologies.

In a digital background defined as work-in-progress, *digitational architecture* represents one of the possible points of perspective to reach a more focused understanding of the dynamics affecting such context. The *Blue Papers* come from this background and belief: they are works in progress of an identity in transition. *Blue Papers* is a collection of academic papers which gather a series of observations regarding architecture in the current age of digitisation and computation. Some of these papers have already been presented in conference proceedings or have been parts of academic activities referring to important institutions and universities—such as the Massachusetts Institute of Technology (MIT), Eidgenössische Technische Hochschule Zürich (ETH Zurich), University College London (UCL), and Politecnico di Milano—while others are published here for the first time. The idea of the entire publication is to collect a series of observations on several topics inside a unique space, a platform where the reader can arbitrarily connect fragments of knowledge developed in different places and at different times. To provide a further element of thought for the combination of a composite reflection, the end of the publication includes a series of projects, theoretical work-in-progress attempts to translate into practice the ideas developed inside the papers. Such projects refer to different types of building and scales, spanning from interior design to private and public buildings, and finally urban design. The reason for this choice is to highlight the possibility to generate a different understanding of an operative architecture in the current age of computation and digitisation through a diversified application of similar principles in different contexts. The ultimate intent of such experimental projects is to stretch the opportunity to combine digital humanities and computational technologies up to their limits: this is the ultimate purpose of this book as preparatory work for future research.

Regarding the papers, the majority of the observations included into them rotate around a broad spectrum of considerations referring to the relationship between architecture and the current digital era, ranging from the problem of authorship and human creativity in computational design to notions related to architectural pedagogy and architectural design and construction. In terms of editorial choice, all the papers preserve the original structure "abstract-content-references" typically used for academic works, reflecting the intent to leave untouched the initial purposes which have led to their conception. The *Blue Papers* are five, and minor changes have been included in those already presented to accommodate new ideas formulated after the original presentation.

The first paper—*Plug-ins Jungle. Algorithmic Design as Inbuilt Dynamism between Human and Artificial Creativity*—has been presented at the conference DESFORM19 organised by the MIT Design Lab at the Massachusetts Institute of Technology, MIT. The paper focuses the attention on new forms of relationship between human and artificial creativity inside the current digital era, in particular referring to algorithmic design and the increasing use and creation of software applications – the so-called plug-ins – rather than traditional monolithic software. Although such an observation might seems exclusively related to a matter of computer science and programming decisions, behind such a shift lies the increasing customisation of computational thinking running in parallel to the contemporary customisation of digital tools. The use of algorithms during the design process has increased exponentially in every design-related discipline, and the creation of new plug-ins is giving birth to a new algorithmic evolution of creativity and a new understanding of the digital society. Interesting enough, in the architectural field, such evolution has also corresponded to the generation of a series of animal-named plug-ins—and the graphical algorithmic editor Grasshopper represents the touchstone of the ongoing creation of a new digital jungle—highlighting the existence of a new dynamic relationship between human and artificial intelligence.

The second paper—*Malleable Authorship in Computational Design. Evolving Digital Anonymity Towards Humanization*—extends the concept of digital anonymity through a closer look to the idea of authorship inside the contemporary age of computation and digitisation. The concept of *digital anonymity* was initially presented at the conference DIGIERA19 organised by the Department of Management, Technology and Economics at ETH Zurich, and later widely revised and included in the scientific journal TECHNE Special Series n.2 (Journal of Technology for Architecture and Environment) published by FUP (Firenze University Press). Regarding the paper *Malleable Authorship in Computational Design*, it was presented for the Digital Humanities Congress 2020 organised by the Digital Humanities Institute at The University of Sheffield (congress postponed to 2021 due to COVID-19). The paper starts by defining the concept of *digital anonymity* and its relationship with human authorship through the use of case studies related to the rising of autonomous, self-generative and self-organising systems. Once exemplified this relationship, the paper analyses more in-depth the matter of authorship in computational design through historical references spanning from the rise of computer-aided design during the 1960s to the more recent developments characterising the current digital turn in architecture. The paper intends to highlight the fact that the evolution of computational design in architecture is irreversibly changing the role of human authorship in design conception and development, and the ongoing shift from human authorship to the computational agency is giving life to new forms of design in response to the new emergent and anonymous digital culture and society. In such a scenario, will human creativity survive the rise of the artificial one or the future of architecture will be designed by artificial intelligence?

The third paper—*Green Robotics. Appraising Robotic Fabrication and Sustainability in Architecture*—looks into the relationship between robotics and sustainability, and it is published here for the first time. The increasing use of computational tools and methods in architecture allows from one side to optimise the design process producing more efficient and performative buildings, while from another side computation represents the central core to programme robots and generate new construction processes based on automation and robotic fabrication. Such a significant evolution of construction processes is producing a series of related effects, and one of them is the rise of new opportunities to improve the efficiency and sustainability of the built environment. In a time where climatic issues represent the core of a new global awareness, rethinking robots as sustainable tools represent one of the possible opportunities to orient the current digital evolution of our society towards a more sustainable—and at the same time technologically advanced—future for the built environment. For this reason, the paper analyses multiple examples in which the use of robotics helps to achieve more efficient and sustainable results in terms of

construction processes and use of resources, pursuing the intent to provide answers to some arising questions such as: what are the possible points
of convergence between robotic fabrication and sustainability? How can
we use computation and robotic fabrication to trace the boundaries of a
green and digital future for architecture? In other words, how green robots can be?

The fourth paper—*Teaching Architecture Without Architects. Architectural
Pedagogy in the Age of Digitisation*—looks into the problem of architectural pedagogy in the current digital era, and it is published here for the first
time. Referring to matters such as the role of the architect and architecture in the contemporary digital society, new teaching methods created
to educate new generations of architects, and the relationship between
teachers and students in the age of computation and digitisation—just
to mention some of the included topics—the paper seeks to analyse the
current relationship between architecture and education prefiguring a
possible perspective for the rise of a practical approach to architectural
teaching. The increasing use of digital technologies and the introduction
of external disciplines related to the new digital reality are giving life to
new forms of education and research methods where the role of teachers
and students is mixed according to a new paratactic tendency dictated by
the rise of digital interdisciplinarity. In such a background of continuous
hybridisation of knowledge, architecture itself and the role of the architect—not only as a professional but as an educator as well—are rapidly
evolving. According to these observations, what is the future of architecture and its education? Will it exclusively become a matter of production
and scientific methods, or it will be able to keep alive in itself the germ of
aesthetic and artistic values of social constructions? In other words, will
the future of architecture be written by architects, or we will witness the
rise of a new architecture without architects?

The fifth and last paper—*Architecture in Connectocracy. Eight Digital Principles for an Operative Architecture*—formulates the concept of *connectocracy* as the power of connection in the current age of digitisation, namely
the perpetual tendency of our time of linking and looking for new sources
of interaction, a new socio-political system characterised by several anthropological implications. Since architecture is first and foremost a matter of social construction, the rise of a contemporary operative architecture must consider any socio-political and anthropological implication
affecting the current digital society and being able to formulate operative
principles coming from it. For this reason, eight digital principles are explained in the paper, and they represent concepts which can be subjectively
understood and re-elaborated inside the design of a possible architecture.
Such principles are connectivity, continuity, decentralisation, immersion,
interface, hyper-textuality, modulation and stratification. In a time where

everything is accessible everywhere at any time, architecture needs an updated conceptual framework able to prevent any passive disengagement in a background of genuine interdisciplinarity. Therefore, the eight principles explained in the paper represent theoretical outposts propaedeutic to the design and construction of an operative architecture.

The definition of *connectocracy* and the formulation of eight operative principles represents the theoretical introduction to the final part of the publication constituted by prototypical projects. These projects represent the practical continuation of concepts and ideas developed inside the previous papers. All the *projects* have to be intended as works reflecting the current state of a more extensive intellectual work currently under construction. These projects are four, and they are ordered according to their scale—from interior design to architectural and urban design.

The first project—*Primitive Voxels*—has been presented at The Bartlett School of Architecture as final work for the module Morphogenetic Programming, which is part of the currently ongoing studies conducted inside the B-Pro MSc Architectural Computation. The project is based on an algorithm that combines particle growth systems and mesh optimisation procedures for the generation of continuous and immersive spaces, and it is part of a research project which intends to investigate the formation of deconstructive spaces converting their nature of "signature spaces" into autonomous mesh configurations generated by computational processes. In doing so, the algorithmic procedure transforms the deconstructive space into voxelated spaces, and after that, autonomous assemblies and non-pedigreed spaces are generated. The use of the adjective "non-pedigreed" related to architecture refers to research conducted in the field of primitive settlements and constructions, a time where architects did not exist and the built environment was shaped by the work of anonymous builders. Nowadays, in the current digital era, computers can be considered as the most prominent of such anonymous builders, and computational procedures lead towards similar although asymmetrical anonymous results.

The second project—*Maison de Cubes*—extends the scale of the investigation field from interior spaces to building structures, from interior design to architectural design. The project is based on an algorithmic procedure that combines structural topology optimisation with voxelisation algorithms. The title of the project refers to Le Corbusier's Maison Dom-Ino, which has been used as the starting point of the computational process. The *Maison de Cubes* optimises the structural elements which constitute the original parts of the Maison Dom-Ino, achieving the same structural performance by using around half the amount of concrete through the use of targeted topology optimisation. Once all the elements have been optimised, the complexity of the generated mesh is converted into cubes through the use of voxelisation algorithms. The final result is a house in which all the elements are converted into cubes—voxels—giving life to a modular system characterised by a hypertextual language. The *Maison de Cubes* converts the traditional architectural elements—columns and floors —into voxelated volumes acting as structural systems. In doing so, the original principles guiding the Maison Dom-Ino are conceptually stretched and translated into their new digital format; in other words, from mass production of houses able to combine themselves into series like dominoes—such as in Le Corbusier's idea—to mass production of components able to combine themselves into houses like Lego blocks. The principles guiding the Maison Dom-Ino shift their point of reference from distinct architectural elements to homogeneous volumetric parts.

The third project—*Mundaneum of the Digital Knowledge*—represents a further extension of scale in terms of architectural design, reaching up the conception of public buildings. In this case, the starting point is the idea of Mundaneum—initially called *Palais Mondial* ("world palace")—developed by the Belgian lawyers Paul Otlet and Henri La Fontaine at the turn of the 20th century. The Mundaneum was an institution having the purpose of collecting all the world's knowledge under the same roof; in other words, a sort of large container of knowledge where everything was gathered and linked. In this case, the project intends to re-elaborate the holistic idea underlining the original project into a new public building intended as a conglomeration of clusterised digital knowledge. Some of the principles analysed in previous papers—such as stratification and connectivity—are here experimented and stretched up to their limits, giving life to an architectural design where spaces and functions are blended according to the uses promoted by the new digital society, a sort of typological mixology under construction for the formation of a possible architectural machine. The project is generated by an algorithmic procedure based on cellular automaton models and voxelisation algorithms. Initially, main directions are established as starting lines for the initiation of the cellular automaton growth. Once the generic volumetric structure is created, voxelisation algorithms divide the structure into voxels set to a specific size, and then such voxels are replaced by standardised architectural components. In doing so, the final design is composed by a series of equal and stratified components where activities are connected through multiple and heterogeneous paths.

Finally, the last project—*The Paratactic City*—extends the experimentation of the previous projects to the urban scale. The project is based on an algorithmic procedure that combines L-systems with voxelisation algorithms. The entire city is designed by algorithmic processes which dictate buildings location and streets configuration. In doing so, the urban environment generated by computational processes is an anonymous land where the action of robots can easily fit into the construction of a new paratactic urban identity. The result is a series of recursive structures dictating a final urban configuration that can accommodate robotic assembly and automated procedures for the construction of both private and public urban spaces and buildings. *The Paratactic City* is the city of interface and compacted decentralisation, the city of architecture without architects, a place for the rise of a new non-geometrical, data-based architecture, where specific sets of data replace the traditional idea of architecture as a combination of distinct and well-defined social, cultural and political structures. For this reason, *The Paratactic City* represents a work-in-progress idea of architectural parataxis reflecting the anthropological levelling promoted by the current digital society, a phenomenon achievable and understandable through the use of computation, and the belief that robots might become the new anonymous builders of the future basing their independence on the novelty promoted by the new genetic complexity of computational processes.

Nonconclusion: beyond an architecture

In conclusion, it is reasonable to say that there is no conclusion, or at least not a unique one except the single reader's subjective understanding. This publication is not intended to show a well-defined path leading towards a well-defined architecture but rather suggesting the reader to put together the fragments of a scattered and unfinished work. Both papers and projects are outposts of an architectural identity still to come, a built environment designed by both human and artificial intelligence. In a time where the "perfection of means and [clusterisation] of goals" prevent architecture from building its new identity on a unitary foundation of goals, this publication intends to go down to basics, bringing the attention of advanced architectural research back to humanities. There is need to consider the current digital condition affecting architecture as a matter of human progress rather than a mere technological development; otherwise, the risk of having no architecture will be a plausible future scenario.

A wider audience might receive such a risk as a problem internal to the architectural discipline, a complication made by architects for architects. After all, as already noted by others in the past, architecture is becoming a necessity in extinction since it is no longer able to interest anyone: too slow and inefficient to satisfy client's needs; too feeble and faded away to represent the power of institutions symbolically; too far from ordinary people to match their real expectations. Therefore, if nobody cares about architecture, why do we need architecture in the age of computation and digitisation?

Although such a question might seem provocative, it is undeniable that architecture is facing a crucial turning point that will inevitably dictate its future survival. As already clarified at the beginning of the introduction, the current digital era represents an undefined and slippery territory for architecture, a time amazingly fertile but, at the same time, incredibly dispersive due to a bulimic availability of tools and methods promoted by the current digital development. After almost thirty years spent experimenting with such new technological opportunities inside the architectural discipline, it seems appropriate to highlight the current period as a historical moment to overcome the weaknesses of a paradoxical era, stepping back from non-stop technological development and taking different decisions. These decisions have to lead architecture toward an entirely new perspective, starting from considering its traditional and more fundamental nature.

According to the traditional understanding, architecture represents the first state of the art in terms of scale and materiality, a testament of concreteness able to pass on to generations the existence of a heritage. Architecture is not merely a matter of construction, but rather construction in aesthetic evolution. In such aesthetic evolution, uses and functions are not enough to define the features of progressive social constructions. Aesthetic represents the taste of an era, an act of choice concerning what we decide to take from the past and pass on to future generations. If architecture is based on aesthetic and aesthetic is a matter of choice, then architecture can be considered a continuous decision. Today, the most significant risk emerging from the current digital era is the loss of such decision ability due to the illusion of freedom promoted by the Neoliberal development of our current digital society. In a time where we can access anything at any time, we learn new things through the abundance of knowledge rather than the sedimentation of it. It seems that we are progressively losing the ability to decide if something is relevant or not because everything has importance in a digital world where everything is possible; in other words, it seems that we can do everything in one click, apart from thinking.

In a context where active decisions are more feeble and passive autonomy is stronger than ever, architecture struggles to keep any trace of its traditional primacy since such primacy has always been based on the human factor. In fact, the simple etymological analysis of the word "architecture"—which refers to the word "architect", from the Greek "architèkton" = "archè" (referring to the concept of primacy) + "tèkton" (creator)—highlights the fact that architecture has always depended by the work and ideas of its "primary creator", namely the architect. Nowadays, the increasing use of computational tools and methods is giving life to new forms of a dynamic relationship between human and artificial intelligence, an inbuilt dynamism through which the human mind and the machine regularly interact with each other producing unexpected and emergent results. The novelty and emergency of such results rectify the existence of an ongoing process of anonymity underling the current digital evolution of architecture, and in such a context, the traditional primacy of the human being over the entire architectural process is undermined. The question that now arises is quite simple but rather crucial: if such human primacy is undermined, are we still producing architecture? Or perhaps what we are currently doing is something else, something that has the potential to go beyond an architecture?

It is probably too early to provide a comprehensive answer to this question, but it is certainly not too early to conduct further research regarding such a matter. Future works will better clarify the pertinence of the statement.

G Bono | London, 04/01/2021

papers

PLUG-INS JUNGLE

Algorithmic Design as Inbuilt Dynamism Between Human and Artificial Creativity

Paper presented with Pilar Maria Guerrieri at the conference DESFORM19 organised by the MIT Design Lab at the Massachusetts Institute of Technology, MIT.

Keywords: *plug-ins, algorithmic design, human creativity, artificial creativity, design ethic.*

Introduction

In 2014, Andrew A. Smith published his book *Grasshopper Jungle* [1]. Despite being a young adult fiction and coming-of-age novel quite unusual and original for its literary genre, its title sounds particularly familiar if referred to algorithmic design. In fact, the graphical algorithmic editor Grasshopper currently represents one of the most popular and developed algorithmic editors for designers available on the market. Its use is widely spread throughout the majority of design-related disciplines, which are now developing new algorithmic techniques to explore new ideas and opportunities during the design process. The rise of such algorithmic approach is transversally affecting the design process at all its scales, breaking down boundaries between disciplines that were far from each other during the past years. As a matter of fact, from urban design to product design, algorithms are providing new platforms of research contributing to the generation of emergent and autonomous design results.

The popularity of an algorithmic editor such as Grasshopper lies in a series of opportunities that it can provide to its users. First of all, Grasshopper allows the creation of graphical-based algorithms generated by an

Abstract

This paper seeks to define the concept of *plug-ins jungle* as generative background in computational design for new forms of dynamic relationship between human and artificial creativity. This definition will be conducted through the use of theoretical references and practical case studies with the intent to show that the current evolution of a *plug-ins jungle* is affecting design results at all its scales—from product design to urban design—and at all its stages—from design conception to construction and fabrication.

In the past twenty years, the creation of software applications during the design process has exponentially increased. One of the most interesting examples regarding such matter corresponds to the graphical algorithmic editor Grasshopper and the generation of a series of animal-named plug-ins through which graphically editing the coding process. Grasshopper and its plug-ins represent the touchstone of the ongoing evolution of a new digital jungle in which new software applications are not only augmenting human creativity but also, they are generating new forms of artificial creativity.

The evidence suggests that the increasing use and creation of software applications during the design process are giving birth to new forms of a dynamic relationship between human and artificial intelligence, an inbuilt dynamism through which the human mind and the machine regularly interact with each other producing unexpected and emergent design results.

inductive process that allows the user to connect pre-coded nodes intuitively. Secondly, it allows the user to personally code new scripts through the use of several programming languages such as C#, Python, and VB. Finally, the generation of new and customised plug-ins is then promoted inside a unique platform in which plug-ins themselves can interact with each other. The inbuilt connection with a 3D modelling software such as Rhinoceros ultimately provides the user with the opportunity to physically produce the designed object through several production techniques, such as the creation of STL files for 3D printing or specific scripts to program robotic arms.

The innovation which this approach is bringing into the design process is clear and significant, and it is giving life to new forms of relationship between human and artificial creativity. These new forms of evolution require an analysis able to consider algorithms not only as mere mathematical tools, but rather as examples of the rise of new human progress in design conception based on the influence of artificial intelligence over the human mind and perception. Nowadays, the interaction between human and artificial intelligence represents an open field of debate and investigation, and Max Tegmark has well depicted such ongoing discussion about people in favour of or against one side or the other in his book *Life 3.0. Being Human in the Age of Artificial Intelligence* [2]. In such a background of interest and research, a series of questions arise: what is the nature of this new relationship between human and artificial intelligence? How is it affecting the design process and the new forms of creativity generated from it?

The answer to these questions requires the use of two concepts, one theoretical and one practical. The former is related to the theoretical point of view to adopt in evaluating the relationship between human and artificial creativity, while the latter refers to the practical ways through which such relationship is manifesting itself. The first concept is the concept of inbuilt dynamism between human and artificial intelligence, while the second one corresponds to the idea of *plug-ins jungle*. Since the former represents the theoretical point of view through which looking at the latter, a note on the inbuilt dynamism between human and artificial creativity is required before explaining the factors which are influencing the rise of the current *plug-ins jungle*.

Note on the inbuilt dynamism between human and artificial creativity

The expression "inbuilt dynamism" refers to the analysis done by the cognitive scientist Margaret Boden in regards to the work of Harold Cohen and his AI system AARON, one of the first example of computer-generated art developed by the British artist during the 1970s. Commenting on Cohen's work and developing the same theoretical construction in her book *The Creative Mind. Myths and Mechanisms* [3], Boden highlights the fact that computational processes—including scripts, frames and semantic nets—are helpful to understand how the brain works and how some aspects of human creativity are possible. The reason for it is "because symbolic and representational structures and transformations are the focus of computer programming, the essence of creativity may not be so far removed from computational processes as is usually assumed" [4]. Although the exitance of similitudes between the human brain and computer was something already well presented in the studies of computational pioneers such as Alan Turing and John Von Neuman [5], Boden provides an interesting interpretative key through which reading such complementary relation between artificial and human intelligence:
    A functioning program has its own inbuilt dynamism. Its activities can be both flexible and constrained, and a proper amalgam of flexibility and constraint is central to creative intelligence. [4]

Then, flexibility and constraint as the two main factors to understand the real measure of complementarity between artificial and human intelligence, a balance that can only be fully appreciated through the awareness of their inbuilt dynamism. Kostas Terzidis provides another important contribution to the idea of dynamic complementarity between human and artificial creativity. In his book *Algorithmic Architecture,* Terzidis focuses the attention on the new computational process in architecture, describing the use of algorithms not only as mere step-by-step problem-solving procedures but rather as ontological constructions with philosophical and sociological repercussions. Starting from clarifying the distinction between computation and computerisation—something already well explained by the author in his previous publication talking about "algorithmic form" [6]—Terzidis coined the term "algotecture" to highlight the use of algorithms in architecture. Proceeding through the explanation of a brief history of such "algotecture" as something substantially different from the more common Computer-Aided Design system—the former not necessarily dependent on the computer, while the latter dependent by definition on it—Terzidis gives evidence to the fact that there are certain levels of problems which cannot be solved by standard CAD systems, but their complexity inevitably required the use of algorithms. His words are particularly significant in this regard:

There are some problems whose complexity, level of uncertainty, ambiguity, or range of possible solutions required a synergic relationship between the human mind and a computer system. Such synergy is possible only through the use of algorithmic strategies that ensure a complementary and dialectic relationship between the human mind and the machine. [7]

Such "complementary and dialectic relationship between the human mind and the machine" highlighted by Terzidis explains the role of algorithmic design in comparison with human creativity through a critical point of view which can be reasonably reconducted to Boden's concept of inbuilt dynamism in functioning programs and their creative intelligence. This critical point of view is based on mutual persuasion and compromises, which can generate new forms of creative dynamism inbuilt in the new artificial dimension of human creativity.

The analysis of these theoretical references has been conducted with the purpose to clarify the complementary relationship between human and artificial creativity. This point of view represents the foundation upon which looking at algorithmic design and evaluating the results coming from it. The ongoing phenomenon of the mathematisation of the design process is based on the creation of software applications, and this approach is characterising the most advanced research in contemporary design. New plug-ins are created and grouped inside more comprehensive platforms—such as Grasshopper—and sometimes they are even programmed to be stand-alone applications. Both cases represent the evidence of an exponentially increasing plug-ins background that is progressively evolving the traditional conception of human design. In such a context, the *plug-in jungle* represents the vast and open landscape in which the collaboration between human and artificial intelligence is emerging and evolving.

Plug-ins jungle

The expression *plug-ins jungle* refers to AD Profile 222 *Computation Works. The Building of Algorithmic Thought* guest-edited by Brady Peters and Xavier De Kestelier in 2013. Inside the issue, a series of examples are presented to analyse the effects of computational design inside the architectural discipline. In the article *Design Eco-System. Customising the Architectural Design Environment with Software Plug-ins*, Daniel Davis and Brady Peters describe the evolution of architectural design towards the use of scripting and personalised plug-ins:

This defines an entirely new landscape in which "cathedrals" (monolithic applications) are challenged by "bazaars" (generative-modelling editors) populated by animal-named plug-ins. [8]

In the following pages, a series of Grasshopper plug-ins are described, such as Kangaroo, Pachyderm Acoustic Simulation, Weaverbird, Geco, Firefly. If now we add to them other Grasshopper plug-ins—such as Goat or Bowerbird, just to mention a couple—and even stand-alone software such as Rhinoceros and its rendering extensions—Penguin or Flamingo among the others—the definition of a *plug-ins jungle* seems pertinent and appropriate for a computational environment dominated by animal-named applications.

Inside the same AD Profile 222, a series of case studies are proposed with the purpose to highlight the effects of such algorithmic tools over the final design results. In this regard, particularly interesting are the examples explained by Giulio Piacentino and the use of the Grasshopper plug-in WeaverBird [9], and Thomas Grabner and Ursula Frick and the use of another Grasshopper plug-in such as GECO [10]. In the first case, the use of the plug-in gives access to surface subdivisions and transformation operators, which allow topological editing of the starting design creation. In doing so, the exploration of a series of design options comes from the action performed by the algorithm itself, which therefore becomes a fundamental factor in design creation. In the second case, the use of the plug-in GECO in conjunction with the software Autodesk Ecotect allows constant interaction between modelling and software analysis, and such interaction produces effects in terms of design results—such as the case study analysed in the article, namely the Shenzhen Border Station competition entry designed by SPAM, where the plug-in has been used to run a solar access analysis through which roof openings have been located and designed. In both cases, the use of plug-ins significantly influences the final design results. Therefore, they are clear examples of how the action of a new *plug-ins jungle* is the touchstone of the rising phenomenon of hybridisation between human and artificial intelligence in the current evolution of creativity in computational design.

The examples which can be mentioned to confirm such fundamental influence of plug-ins over final design results are numerous and significant. Nowadays, the use of Grasshopper and its plug-ins is becoming part of the standard practice in many architectural firms, and it is very often the case to see such applications embedded into standard workflows from the very early stages of the design process, representing essential tools of design exploration and optimisation. The concept of *plug-ins jungle* goes far beyond being a definition related to a single algorithmic editor such as Grasshopper, but rather it represents a more complex working model towards which both the design profession and the construction industry are evolving too. Algorithmic procedures and software applications constitute by now the core of any advanced research related to the built environment, and this aspect represents an explicit confirmation of the fact that the ongoing process of mathematisation is not only producing new forms of evolution inside the single discipline but more importantly, it is linking together different disciplines inside new algorithmic platforms.

Extended examples of plug-ins jungle

In the current evolution of computational design, there are several fields of research in which the action of the *plug-ins jungle* plays a central role in the realisation of final design results. First of all, *plug-ins jungle* is the natural habitat for the complexity of design generated in the last twenty years across all design-related disciplines. Promoted by the rise of a mass-customised production system, sophisticated software applications and new digital fabrication technologies have enabled designers to build experimental structures with high levels of complexity. Such complexity is based on continuous and seamless forms, and although nowadays such trend seems to be overtaken by the rise of a more discrete approach— in this regards, Lei Zheng offers an interesting comparison between the two models [11]—the digital turn of design in the last two decades has been based on a constant exploration of complex shapes and structures. For instance, the work conducted at ZHACODE is particularly significant in this regard. The computation and design group at Zaha Hadid Architects is a research group that focuses its attention on invention and innovation through the use of computer software programming and physical computing, considering algorithms as exploratory phases for the discovery of new design and production opportunities. Among a wide range of projects, the installation Thallus exhibited in Milan during Salone del Mobile 2017 represents a perfect example of the research conducted by ZHACODE in terms of customisation and mechanisation of the design process. The installation is composed of a 7-kilometre-long continuous line made of an extruded structural strip produced by 6-axis robotic 3D printing technology. The design of the structural strip is based on differential growth methods dictated by an algorithm that uses specific parameters—such as proximity to boundaries, angled direction of the ruling, and structural requirements—to establish density gradation and direction of growth.

Other than representing the field of action for complex forms and structures in digital mass-customised production, the *plug-ins jungle* is also the place for creating tools through which promoting open-source design. The rise of open-ended and adaptable systems based on sharing software, ideas and models is becoming one of the main fields of research in the current evolution of computational design across all disciplines. An interesting example of this approach is represented by the work done by Enriqueta Llabres and Eduardo Rico in terms of urban analysis and design. Through their multidisciplinary London-based office Relational Urbanism, Llabres and Rico developed a design approach to digital configurations of urban documentation based on Relational Urban Models (RUMs). As explained by the authors in their article *Relational Urban Models: Parameters, Values and Tacit Forms of Algorithms* [12], RMUs are design models based on new forms of digital urban documents which collect inputs from designers, government bodies and members of the public, allowing information sharing and feedback from the end-user to the design team and vice versa. This new form of shared authorship in design conception is possible through an application based on a generative algorithm able to analyse data and parameters to elaborate on new urban configurations. For instance, parameters based on the proximity of the street network allow the retention of certain blocks and the removal of certain others, or again the final configuration of a tower can be sculpted by constraints of sunlight exposure. The final design is the result of the action of algorithms able to mediate the effects of environmental parameters with the starting requirements coming from human inputs.

Another field of research in which the *plug-ins jungle* plays an important role is automation and robotic fabrication. For example, the extensive use of 6-axis robotic arms in design production and assembly is made possible by the use of algorithms and software applications, which not only allow to program robots according to specific design requirements but also influence the final design results through the control of the robot's action and movement. For instance, the Grasshopper plug-in Robots—developed by Vicente Soler—is a clear example of this process, and it allows to program several types of robots—such as ABB, KUKA and UR robots. Always talking about robotic fabrication and the influence on design played by algorithms to program such machines, an interesting example is provided by heterogeneous multi-robot systems, which constitute an open field of research at the ICD/ITKE at the University in Stuttgart. As explained by Maria Yablonina and Achim Menges [13], such multi-robot systems are based on the use of bespoke design machines in conjunction with standard industrial robots. This mix during the fabrication process allows a higher level of flexibility and scalability compared to the exclusive use of industrial robotic arms. An example of this process is provided by the ICD/ITKE Research Pavilion 2016-17. In this case, the use of a path correction algorithm relying on a camera-based tracking system controls the flight of the mobile robot, which is represented by an unmanned aerial vehicle (UAV). In contrast, other software applications are used to analyse and optimise the Pavilion structure, dictating robots' movement through the location of the primary and secondary structures, both made of carbon tensile filament structures with the primary one realised in carbon fibre-reinforced ribs.

Finally, another field of research in which the action of the *plug-ins jungle* plays an essential role in the creation of final design results is represented by optimisation and form-finding techniques. As explained by Mark Burry describing the works of Antoni Gaudí and Frei Otto as main precursors in computational design in terms of form-finding and structural optimisation [14], today such techniques are widely used in contemporary design conception, and they are based on several software applications. For instance, Kangaroo is one of the most popular plug-ins for Grasshopper, and its use allows modification of the design in response to engineering analyses simulating aspects of the behaviour of real-world materials and objects. Always regarding such matter, the work of the Digital Structures research group at the MIT Massachusetts Institute of Technology represents a prominent example in terms of structural optimisation and the different design configuration generated from it. Group leader Caitlin Mueller pays particular attention to the relationship between structural optimisation and design conception in her article *Distributed Structures: Digital Tools for Collective Design* [15]. Highlighting the fact that the creation of new computational tools is shifting the role of computation itself from representation and analysis to creative idea generation, Mueller provides a series of examples in which the use of multi-objective optimisation techniques offers the opportunity for the designer to choose between different options generating during the optimisation process. Such opportunities are made possible by the use of plug-ins developed explicitly for such purpose. For instance, the web-based design application StructureFIT and the Rhino and Grasshopper plug-in Stormcloud—both developed by the MIT Digital Structures research group—allow designers to explore new design typologies and forms with a high level of structural feasibility.

The examples described so far represent only four instances belonging to a wide range of case studies in which the final design is the result of a very close relationship between the human input and the computational calculation belonging to the machine. From this relationship, a new design world is rising, and the *plug-ins jungle* represents its natural habitat. Such habitat is based on the constant interaction between the human mind and the machine, which affects design right at the very beginning of its conception. Within this context, plug-ins are the places able to host new forms of emergent creativity coming from a new relationship between the human being and the computational machine.

Conclusion

The theoretical observations and practical case studies analysed so far represent a critical point of view through which looking at the current evolution of computational design and the increasing use of software applications during the design process. The rise of the *plug-ins jungle* is affecting computational design at every scale—from product to urban design—and at all its stages—from design conception to automated fabrication. Software applications are becoming an indispensable prerequisite for any design process, and the fact that the authorial role of the human designer may not survive to this digital turn is a real possibility for the future of any design-related profession. As already explained by Mario Carpo in his book *The Alphabet and the Algorithm*, the frequent use of algorithms may eventually transform human designers into IT developers, i.e., changing their role from creators to mere plug-ins users/generators [16]. This scenario may not represent an alarming point for those who believe that the future will not belong to human beings but computational machines. On the other hand, this perspective may not be supported by those who believe that any technological development is, first and foremost, a matter of human progress.

The theoretical construction of the entire paper is built upon the relationship between two different subjects—such as the human being and the computational machine—and the inbuilt dynamism which regulates such relationship. Considering the design process as a field of investigation has constituted an appropriate point of view to understand the dynamic complementarity between such entities and the creativity which arises from them. After all, as already explained by Nicholas Negroponte at the very beginning of the computational evolution of design:

The partnership is not one of master (smart, leader) and slave (dumb, follower), but rather of two associates which each have the potential for self-improvement [...]. Eventually, a separation of the parts could not occur; the entire 'symbiotic' system would be, as Gordon Pask described, an artificial intelligence that cannot be partitioned. [17]

According to Negroponte, from the rise of this new form of artificial intelligence, a new "extended designer" (the human being) and "artificial designer" (the computational machine) will be generated in favour of a constant and mutual design complementation, augmentation, and inter-action between human beings and machines. Today, such extended de-signer and artificial designer are two actors of the same reality, and their interaction is continuously producing new forms of inbuilt dynamism be-tween human and artificial intelligence. The complementary approach be-tween them seems to be a more appropriate point of view from which look-ing at the ongoing evolution of algorithmic design, and a closer look into its natural habitat, namely a walk into the *plug-ins jungle,* may provide a valid starting point for further research.

[1]   Smith, A., *Grasshopper Jungle*, Penguin Books, 2014.

[2]   Tegmark, M., *Life 3.0. Being Human in the Age of Artificial Intelligence*, Penguin Books, 2017, 31.

[3]   Boden, M., *The Creative Mind. Myths and Mecha-nisms*, Weidenfeld and Nicolson, 1990.

[4]   Boden, M., "Creativity and computers", in *Har-old Cohen* (exhibition catalogue), The Tate Gal-lery, 1983, 17-8.

[5]   Von Neuman, J., *The Computer and the Brain*, Yale University Press, 1958.

[6]   Terzidis, K., "Algorithmic Form", in *Expressive Form*, Spon Press, 2003, 65-75.

[7]   Terzidis, K., *Algorithmic Architecture*, Elsevi-er Architectural Press, 2006, 37.

[8]   Davis, D. and Peters, B., "Design Eco-System. Customizing the Architectural Design Environ-ment with Software Plug-Ins", in Peters, B. and De Kestelier, X. (Ed.), *Computational Works. The Building of Algorithmic Thought*, AD Profile 222 (March-April 2013), 125.

[9]   Piacentino, G., "WeaverBird. Topological mesh editing for architects", in Peters, B. and De Kestelier, X. (Ed.), *Computational Works. The Building of Algorithmic Thought*, AD Profile 222 (March-April 2013), 140-1.

[10] Grabner, T. and Frick, U., "GECO. Architectural Design Through Environmental Feedback", in Pe-ters, B. and De Kestelier, X. (Ed.), *Computation-al Works. The Building of Algorithmic Thought*, AD Profile 222 (March-April 2013), 142-3.

[11] Zheng, L. "Meta-Utopia and the Box. Two Sto-ries about Avant-Garde Projects", in Retsin, G. (Ed.), *Discrete. Reappraising the Digital in Ar-chitecture*, AD Profile 258 (March-April 2019), 130-5.

[12] Llabres, E. and Rico, E., "Relational Urban Mod-els. Parameters, Values and Tacit Forms of Al-gorithms", in Schumacher, P. (Ed.), *Parametri-cism 2.0. Rethinking Architecture's Agenda for the 21st Century*, AD Profile 240 (March-April 2016), 84-91.

[13] Yablonina, M. and Menges, A., "Distributed Fab-rication. Cooperative Making with Larger Groups of Smaller Machines", in Retsin, G., *Discrete. Reappraising the Digital in Architecture*, AD Profile 258 (March-April 2019), 62-9.

[14] Burry, M., "Antoni Gaudí and Frei Otto. Essen-tial Precursors to the Parametricism Manifes-to", in Schumacher, P. (Ed.), *Parametricism 2.0. Rethinking Architecture's Agenda for the 21st Century*, AD Profile 240 (March-April 2016), 30-5.

[15] Mueller, C., "Distributed Structures. Digital Tools for Collective Design", in Tibbits, S. (Ed.), *Autonomous Assembly. Designing for a New Era of Collective Construction*, AD Profile 248 (July-August 2017), 94-103.

[16] Carpo, M., *The Alphabet and the Algorithm*, The MIT Press, 2011, 126-7.

[17] Negroponte, N., "Towards a Humanism through Ma-chines", in *Architectural Design*, n. 7/6 (Sep-tember 1969), 511-2.

MALLEABLE AUTHORSHIP IN COMPUTATIONAL DESIGN

Evolving Digital Anonymity Towards Humanisation

Paper accepted for the Digital Humanities Congress 2020 organised by the Digital Humanities Institute at The University of Sheffield (conference postponed to 2021 due to COVID-19).

Keywords: *architecture, artificial intelligence, authorship, computational design, virtual partnership*

Introduction: about digital anonymity

The evolution of computational design is significantly changing the identity of architecture and the role of the architect during its creation. Such evolution cannot be reduced to mere technological development, but first and foremost, it is a matter of human progress. For this reason, considering the traditional concept of human authorship instead of the contemporary one represented by computational agency reflects the intention to look at the current evolution of computational design through a humanistic point of view, an alternative approach to use and to evaluate the wide variety of computational tools and possibilities not only as mere users, but first of all, as active creators of a new digital culture and society.

Among a series of effects emerging in such computational background, *digital anonymity* [1] appears to be one of the most distinctive. *Digital anonymity* is defined as the autopoietic condition of digital design, a state in which the combination of decontextualisation and depersonalisation of the design process leads towards emergent and anonymous

Abstract

This paper seeks to define the concept of *malleable authorship* as a new condition of human authorship in computational design applied to architecture. Starting from the idea of *digital anonymity* as the autopoietic condition of digital design which leads towards emergent and anonymous design results, the concept of *malleable authorship* represents the flexible condition of human authorship in the new architectural background, namely a new level of human flexibility and adaptability in design authorship in response to the rise of computational agency and the evolution of artificial intelligence.

The paper starts by defining the concept of *digital anonymity* and its relationship with human authorship through the use of case studies related to the rising of autonomous, self-generative and self-improving systems. Once exemplified this relationship, the paper analyses more in-depth the matter of authorship in computational design through historical references spanning from the rise of computer-aided design during the 1960s to the more recent developments characterising the current digital turn in architecture.

The evidence suggests that the evolution of computational design in architecture is irreversibly changing the role of human authorship in design conception and development, and the ongoing shift from human authorship to computational agency is giving life to new forms of design in response to the new emergent and anonymous digital culture and society.

design results. The complexity of our present builds its foundation upon an evolutionary process characterised by a "speed of evolution" [2] able to promote a progressive loss of any sedimentary process in favour of disengaged assimilation of knowledge. Inside such a context, the generative capability of the algorithm in architecture and the emergence of creativity introduced into the design process through mathematical computation give life to a new autopoietic condition in which design can potentially reproduce itself autonomously. The traditional design approach based on acquisition, sedimentation, and reinvention of knowledge—which characterises the inductive approach of human creativity—is substituted by algorithms that can produce endless variations starting from a given set of data. Such translation is based on the intentional approach, which leads to artificial creativity. In such transformation, the context is condensed into a series of parameters where the intuitive and visionary work of human beings is substituted by endless mathematical combinations coming from the generative capability of algorithms. For this reason, *digital anonymity* is the touchstone of an ongoing evolutionary process that is translating design into its new digital realm transforming the independence of human creativity into the primacy of artificial creativity. In such a transition, design results become more autonomous and human authorship more anonymous.

Examples of digital anonymity and human authorship in computational design

Such dualism between human authorship and artificial agency is still an open field of debate and investigation in the contemporary architectural world. The advancement of computational technologies and the generative capability of algorithms used to develop them are continuously raising new questions about what is human and what is artificial: is the human being creating new forms of design, or the computer is doing the job instead?

The contemporary evolution of autonomous, self-generative, and self-improving systems in architecture provides an appropriate answer to this question. Such evolution is strictly connected to the idea of *digital anonymity*. In the contemporary evolution of computation in architecture, there are several examples to support this idea, more precisely case studies and research that effect design creation at all its scales, from the large scale represented by urban design to the small one constituted by interior and product design.

Swarm systems represent the first example. Swarm systems are processes that involve seeding design intent into a set of autonomous design agents that can self-organise themselves. Such systems can act at different scales, giving life to significant interventions of "Swarm Urbanism" [3] or localised architectural forms of "Swarm-Constructed Architecture" [4], both affecting the role of human authorship and highlighting the prominence of mathematical tools. For the first instance, Neil Leach specifies that "an application of swarm logic to urbanism enables a shift from the notion of the master-plan to that of master-algorithm as an urban design tool" [3: 61]; while in terms of architecture and robotic fabrication, Robert Stuart-Smith says:
This shift design into new roles is able to operate alongside or replace, existing methods, and potentially reinstates the designer as the encoder of autonomous robotic behaviours for the construction of architectures still unknown. [4: 58-9]

The shift from designer to "encoder of autonomous robotic behaviours" is a clear sign of the fact that human authorship is becoming a marginal factor in the creative process which leads to the final design results, confining the human being to the role of the encoder of inputs and parameters through which initialising the true creative process which does not happen inside the human mind, but rather inside the computational machine and its algorithmic procedures.

Cyber-physical production systems represent another interesting example in terms of *digital anonymity* and human authorship. As explained by Achim Menges in his essay *The New Cyber-Physical Making in Architecture Computational Construction* [5], cyber-physical production systems are based on the improved connectivity promoted by the "Fourth Industrial Revolution."[6] They represent a clear example of the increasing ability of computers to self-learn, self-configure, and self-operate. In fact, through a much higher level of integration and cross-linking between the physical and digital domains which characterised the current digital industrial revolution, machines, and robots have started to gain sensing and self-learning capabilities, acquiring new levels of awareness in terms of self-prediction and self-configuration. The rise in new forms of artificial independence is decreasing the primacy of human action and its relevance inside new design models and production systems,conferring to the computational agency the central role of the creator.

Finally, the same autonomy and self-operability highlighted in cyber-physical production systems can be found in another computational example, more precisely aggregate systems and granular morphologies. As explained by the work conducted by Karola Dierichs and Achim Menges [7], in a standard aggregate system, the single component is known. At the same time, the overall granular structure is emergent and unpredictable, more precisely dictated by the mathematical algorithms which govern the generative computational process. For this reason, even if the human designer develops the single particle's morphology, the general formation remains tendential and probabilistic. The shift of the human designer to the role of "forecaster of possible spatial and structural formations" [7: 87] represents another clear example of the progressive loss of human authorship in computational design and the consequent rise of new autonomous systems based on the generative capability of algorithms.

Authorship, ownership, and virtual partnership

As explained by the examples mentioned so far, new levels of autonomy and independence of artificial systems are putting at stake the traditional conception of human authorship in architectural design, focusing the attention of computational agency as a substitute of the former. For this reason, computational design is profoundly influencing the nature of human authorship giving life to new levels of flexibility and adaptability never experienced before, particulalry in terms of customisation of thinking.

Having highlighted the fact that there is an ongoing phenomenon of anonymity that is influencing the evolution of computational design, how is it possible to ensure that human authorship is disappearing in this anonymous reality? After all, human inputs still represent the starting point of any computational process, and they are vital factors to set rules and data upon which any computational calculation generates and evolves. For this reason, isn't it perhaps more appropriate suggesting the idea that the nature of human authorship is evolving towards a more adaptable and flexible identity rather than completely disappearing? To answer this question, a closer look at the nature of authorship in contemporary computational design is required to understand the inbuilt dynamism between human and artificial creativity which lies underneath any computational creation.

First of all, the role of authorship and ownership in the contemporary digital world has always constituted a source of debates and observations. Significant contributions regarding such topic have been collected by Antoine Picon and Wendy W Fok in their guest-edited AD Profile 243 *Digital Property. Open-Source Architecture* [8]. Discussing the convergence in architecture towards the possibility of a genuinely open sourced approach based on sharing software, ideas and models, regarding the concepts of authorship and ownership, Picon and Fok immediately specify the fact that "whereas authorship used to be the main concern of the architect, ownership is becoming a more and more central question" [8: 7-8]. In an open sourced architectural context, the fact that ownership assumes a central role in the creation of architectural results lies in the increasing level of virtual partnership between the human starting idea and the influence of artificial intelligence and its autonomy. Tristan Gobin, Sebastian Andraos, and Thibault Schwartz provide an interesting point of view regarding such matter:
    With the use of common language, and then access to countless tools, the role of architects becomes increasingly diluted by their computational aids. [...] "As the machinery grows in flexibility and initiative, this association between humans and machines will be more properly described as a partnership", and there are inevitably questions as the responsibility, ethics, insurance and legislation of algorithms surrounding this topic. [9: 72-3]

The "diluted role" of the architect and the rising of a more rooted partnership between human and artificial intelligence are symptoms of a radical ongoing change in the architectural profession, and the fact that the architect's authorship is mutating its nature influenced by the increasing level of artificial autonomy. Such observations require answers able to set a new role for architects in the current evolution of computational design and the nature of their contribution, namely the new measure of their authorship. Understanding such measure represents a crucial point to trace authentic digital progress in architecture, namely giving life to a new compositional approach which can design and consider architecture not only as a mere result of mathematical calculations but rather as a distinctive feature of human progress.

The meaning of the author and its evolution in architecture

The use of the word "progress"—rather than "development"—is not a coincidence, but rather an intention to focus the attention on the humanistic part which lies underneath every technological development. Since the attention now is focused on human authorship in the contemporary digital world, the first point to clarify is what an author is. In this regard, Michel Foucault provides a remarkable definition:

The author is the principle of thrift in the proliferation of meaning. [...] He is a certain functional principle by which, in our culture, one limits, excludes, and chooses; in short, by which one impedes the free circulation, the free manipulation, the free composition, decomposition, and re-composition of fiction. [10: 119]

In describing the author as a functional principle, Foucault clarifies the fact that scientific—and then technological—evolution has always been a detrimental element in terms of human authorship. If during the rise of the Western civilisation the author was received as a statement of demonstrated truth—for instance, in describing ancient principles, we frequently use expressions such as "Aristotle says" or "Plato says"—a change of the author function occurred during the 17th and 18th centuries in conjunction with the rise of the scientific discourse. In such scientific evolution, anonymity began to increase as a consequence of an always re-demonstrable truth. The previous vision of the author as stated truth faded away, and the idea of the scientific inventor "replaced it served only to christen a theorem, proposition, particular effect, property, body, group of elements, or pathological syndrome" [10: 199].

For Foucault, such scientific influence to authorship leads toward the complete disappearance of the human author in favour of the rise of new forms of anonymity to be determined or experienced case-by-case, more precisely what he calls "anonymity of a murmur."

Foucault's prophecy of transforming the author in an "anonymity of a murmur" does not sound unfamiliar if considered the contemporary digital turn in architecture. As previously highlighted talking about *digital anonymity* and the contemporary evolution of autonomous, self-generative, and self-improving systems in architecture, the rise of computational design is shifting the primacy of human authorship in architecture in favour of the generative capacity of the computational agency. Interesting enough, such a process does not represent something entirely new for the architectural discipline, but rather it is rooted inside a historical process started a long time ago.

Regarding this matter, Mario Carpo provides a historical perspective in his book *The Alphabet and The Algorithm* [11]. Referring to one of the critical practices of modernity in architecture—the making of identical copies—Carpo analyses the meaning of authorship in architecture starting from the Renaissance and "the transition from Brunelleschi's artisanal authorship ("this building is mine because I made it") to Alberti's intellectual authorship ("the building in mine because I designed it")" [11: 22-6]. Once specified the ideal view of authorship promoted by Alberti, Carpo focuses the attention on the mass production of copies coming from mechanical master models during the industrial revolution. Then he extends this historical perspective to the current digital turn in architecture. In this regard, he says:

As the digital turn is reshaping the Albertian and modern terms of architectural agency, and architects adjust to a new and unstated authorial environment, many transitional hybrids between the old model and the new are likely to be tried out. [...] And soon, designers will have to choose. They may design objects, and then be digital interactors. Or they may design objectiles, and then be digital authors. [...] To embrace digital authorship in full. However, designers will need to rise to the challenge of a new, digitally negotiated, partially indeterminacy in the process of making form. [...] The modern process of architectural design, and the architect's authorial role in it, may not survive the digital turn. [11: 126-7]

In Carpo's theoretical construction, the fact that the authorial role of the architect may not survive the digital turn is a real possibility for the future of the profession. The advent of computational design and the more frequent use of algorithms in architecture may transform architects into IT developers changing their role from creators to mere plug-ins users/generators. The previously explained Foucault's prophecy of transforming the author in an "anonymity of a murmur" seems then be transposed into the architectural discipline by Carpo's analysis, namely moving the point of view from the "anonymity of a murmur" to the anonymity of an architectural algorithm.

When the author goes digital

Carpo's analysis and critical construction bring our attention to the digitisation of authorship as an ongoing process in contemporary architecture, an incontrovertible phenomenon that is changing the profession and the design generated from it.

The phenomenon of digitisation of authorship in architecture grows and expands from the very beginning of the introduction of computer in the architectural discipline, namely during the 1960s [12]. Nicholas Negroponte represents an essential reference for the evolution of computer-aided design in architecture, and interesting enough, he pays particular attention to the aspects of the new humanistic aspects promoted by the advent of the new computational world.

In his seminal book *The Architecture Machine* [13], Negroponte highlights the fact that the final goal for the introduction of computer-aided design in architecture is to give life to a new humanism through the machine, more precisely a cohabitation and a perfect symbiosis between human and artificial intelligence to avoid any phenomenon of dehumanisation. Negroponte focuses his attention on declaring the paratactic and complementary relationship between the human being and the machine. In doing so, he highlights the primary importance of humanisation over mechanisation, more precisely the adoption of a critical point of view from which the new digital evolution is not seen as mere technological development but as the driving force of human progress. The rise of computational design causes undeniable repercussions in terms of the human psyche and behaviour, and such influential aspects represent critical factors for the definition of a new horizon for the architectural discipline and profession. Negroponte's "architecture machine" is a comprehensive and profoundly influential partner of the human work, and this close relationship produces an inevitable effect in terms of human authorship:

As soon as the designer furnishes the machine with instructions for finding a method of solution, the authorship of the results become ambiguous. Whenever a mechanism is equipped with a processor capable of finding a method 'of finding a method of the solution', the authorship of the answer probably belongs to the machine. If we extrapolate this argument, eventually the machine's creativity will be as separable from the designer's initiative as our designs and actions are from the pedagogy of our grandparents. [13: 111]

Besides highlighting the close relationship between the human being and the machine, Negroponte sees the rise of a new level of autonomy and independence of the latter over the former. Nevertheless, once again, his point of view is ethical rather than merely technological. Such artificial self-controlled evolution involves significant changing in terms of human creativity and the prominence of human authorial work over the rising level of novelty and complexity promoted by artificial creativity.

Conclusion: towards a malleable authorship

Negroponte's words and the other references and examples analysed so far rectify the fact that computational design is irreversibly changing the nature of human authorship giving life to new levels of flexibility and adaptability in terms of authorial work. The rise of *digital anonymity* is putting at stake the traditional primacy of authorship, and the action of the computational agency is setting the boundaries of a new level of human authorship in digital design. Creativity is becoming an open horizon in which human beings and machines are continually interacting, and the frequency and regularity of such interactions are constantly raising questions about the primacy of human creativity over the artificial one and vice versa.

Max Tegmark has well depicted the ongoing debate about people in favour of or against one side or the other in his book *Life 3.0. Being Human in the Age of Artificial Intelligence* [14]. According to Tegmark's theoretical construction, there are three distinct schools of thoughts: "digital utopians, techno-skeptics and members of the beneficial-AI movement" [14: 31]. Using such distinction, at the moment we can reasonably say that being "techno-skeptics" simply means denying the present, and refusing the present certainly does not provide an appropriate starting point for building any future. On the other hand, it is still probably too early to be "digital utopians." Eventually, there are good chances that the synthetic approach underlying the current evolution of AL will overtake the simulation approach referring to AI, but this is going to take a certain amount of time, most likely in the order of several generations. For this reason, at the current stage of human progress, it is more appropriate to be "members of the beneficial-AI movement", namely believing in an equalitarian and complementary relationship between the human being and the machine.

In such a contemporary background, human authorship can evolve if the human being will be able to accept a more malleable nature of his work. Nowadays, being a designer means being able to adopt a flexible and adaptable approach in facing design problems, namely being able to lose any pre-acquired design idea in favour of case-by-case research continually starting from scratch. Only in this way, such research will be able to adopt a critical point of view genuinely authentic and able to propose appropriate solutions concerning the needs of the current era. Constant criticism is a fundamental prerequisite in an era like the digital one which is evolving under the action of perpetual progress where changes and mutations happen on a daily basis.

In this environment of constant evolution, human authorship can only survive if it will be able to reflect its context of reference, namely becoming more flexible, adaptable, malleable; in other words, being able to shape itself according to always new points of research and investigation. Like a metal can be beaten into a sheet without breaking or cracking, authorship can be influenced and made pliable without necessarily being lost. It is only a matter of being aware of the existence of a new level of human authorship, more precisely, the existence of *malleable authorship*.

In a way, the malleability of authorship is a prerequisite in computational design, and this aspect is due to the use of algorithms. As already explained by Kostas Terzidis through his construction of a new "algotecture", algorithms have their generative capacity, and such "intellectual power of an algorithm lies in its ability to infer new knowledge and to extend certain limits of the human intellect" [15: 65]. Stating the fact that algorithms have an "intellectual power" means to rectify the existence of artificial intelligence and its crucial influence over the human one:

Along the lines of *homo faber homo fabricates* (i.e. we make a tool, and the tool makes us), algorithms can be seen as design tools that lead towards the production of novel concepts, ideas, or forms, which, in turn, have an effect in the way designers think thereafter. [...] The computer becomes a mirror of the human mind, and as such, it reflects its thinking. Therefore, design can be explored as a mental process not only by observing human behavior, but also by observing the machine's behavior. [15: 60]

Then, human and artificial intelligence are nowadays two indivisible entities, and such close bond produces hybrid design results. This constant interconnection is flexible and malleable by definition; therefore, a flexible and malleable attitude in human authorship and creativity is crucial to address this new virtual partnership towards a productive horizon. For this reason, the idea of *malleable authorship* can provide the right level of interaction between human being and machine in computational design, a new perspective in human authorship, perhaps weaker than the previous one but more authentic and appropriate to the current evolution of our digital era.

Once introjecting the existence of artificial intelligence and the rising of artificial creativity in contemporary design, a final consideration is due to clarify that such existence does not necessarily overcome human intelligence and creativity. In his seminal book *An Evolutionary Architecture* [16], John Frazer provides a clear point of view through which looking at the computer and its influence over the human mind. He defines computers "as slaves of infinite power and patience", but also he warns the reader that "computers are not without their dangers. If used unimaginatively, they tend dull critical faculties" [16: 18]. Such consideration reminds us to not forget the uniqueness of critical human faculties, namely the critical point of being human. Only through such criticism it is possible to elevate the generative capability of computational design and channelise its development through an authentic architecture of human progress. Although fully digital, such evolution will not be virtual but somehow real and tangible. In such a new digital context, the human being will still be there, still the author of the present reality and the upcoming future, but only under one condition: accepting the hybrid nature of his authorship in the new digital era, its flexibility and malleability; in other words, becoming aware of the rising of *malleable authorship*.

[1] Bono, G. and Guerrieri, P., "Digital Anonymity. Human-Machine Interaction in Architectural Design", in *TECHNE Special Series n.2* (Journal of Technology for Architecture and Environment), FUP (Firenze University Press), 2020, 177-81.

[2] De Kerckhove, D. and Miranda de Almeida, C., *The Point of Being*, Cambridge Scholars Publishing, 2014, 31.

[3] Leach, N., "Swarm Urbanism", in Leach, N. (Ed.), *Digital Cities*, AD Profile 200 (July-August 2009), 56-63.

[4] Stuart-Smith, R., "Behavioral Production. Autonomous Swarm-Constructed Architecture", in Schumacher, P. (Ed.), *Parametricism 2.0. Rethinking Architecture's Agenda for the 21st Century*, AD Profile 240 (March-April 2016), 54-9.

[5] Menges, A., "The New Cyber-Physical Making in Architecture. Computational Construction", in Menges, A. (Ed.), *Material Synthesis. Fusing the Physical and the Computational*, AD Profile 237 (September-October 2015), 28-33.

[6] Schwab, K., *The Fourth Industrial Revolution*, The Fourth Industrial Revolution, 2016.

[7] Dierichs, K. and Menges, A., "Fabrication Agency", in Menges, A. (Ed)., *Material Synthesis. Fusing the Physical and the Computational*, AD

Profile 237 (September-October 2015), 86-91.

[8] Fok, W. W and Picon, A., "The Ownership Revolution", in Fok, W. W and Picon, A. (Ed.), *Digital Property. Open-Source Architecture*, AD Profile 243 (September-October 2016), 6-15.

[9] Gobin, T., Andraos, S. and Schwartz, T., "An Art of Connectivity", in Fok, W. W and Picon, A. (Ed.), *Digital Property. Open-Source Architecture*, AD Profile 243 (September-October 2016), 68-75.

[10] Foucault, M., "What is an Author", in Rabinow, P. (Ed.), *The Foucault Reader*, Pantheon Books, 1984, 101-20.

[11] Carpo, M., *The Alphabet and the Algorithm*, The MIT Press, 2011.

[12] Howard, R., *Computing in Construction. Pioneers of the Future*, Butterworth Heinemann, 1998.

[13] Negroponte, N., *The Architecture Machine. Toward a More Human Environment*, The MIT Press, 1970.

[14] Tegmark, M., *Life 3.0. Being Human in the Age of Artificial Intelligence*, Penguin Books, 2017.

[15] Terzidis, K., *Algorithmic Architecture*, Elsevier Architectural Press, 2006.

[16] Frazer, J., *An Evolutionary Architecture*, Architectural Association Press, 1995.

GREEN ROBOTICS

Appraising Robotic Fabrication and Sustainability in
Architecture

Unpublished

Keywords: *architecture, computation, construction, robotic fabrication, sustainability.*

Introduction: the global awareness of climate issues

In recent years the global awareness of climate issues has exponentially increased. In the last half-century, around nine trillion tonnes of ice melted from the earth's glaciers, while current estimations suggest that half a trillion tonnes of ice are melting every year [1]. In addition to that, global weather patterns are changing; biodiversity is diminishing; species, habitats and non-renewable resources are expiring. World human population increased by over 4.5 billion in the last sixty years [2]—with a prediction of a further 2.6 billion people by 2050—and 50% of such an increased population lives in poverty with no house or suitable living space. Considering such critical housing needs, the current rate of population growth requires that we build double the quantity of living space over the next 30 years [3].

Although urgent global needs require a rapid increase in productivity inside the construction industry, such an increase has to consider the significant climate issues currently hitting the planet, and therefore developing

Abstract

This paper seeks to analyse the relationship between robotic fabrication and sustainability inside the current state of architecture and the construction industry. Such analysis will be conducted through initial considerations about the contemporary architectural context and then through the use of references considered as appropriate to explain the possible scenario in which robotic fabrication can be employed to solve issues related to the efficiency and sustainability of the built environment.

During the last decade, the relationship between building systems and automation systems has significantly changed. Computation represents the central core to programme robots and generates new construction processes. The development of such new approaches is generating a significant reappraisal of the architectural discipline, and at the same time, is moving the construction industry towards more customised and integrated models where the use of robots acts as a disruptive factor concerning traditional building methods and procedures.

The evidence suggests that the increasing use of computation and robotic fabrication is giving life to new models and methods to create more sustainable and efficient construction processes. Rethinking robots as sustainable tools represents one of the possible perspectives to orient the current digital evolution of our society towards a more sustainable and technologically advanced future.

the entire sector towards more sustainable approaches and methods is paramount. The construction industry is one of the largest industrial sectors in the world economy, representing up to 13% of the global GDP and employing around 7% of the world population [4]. It is also the industry with the broader global consumer of raw materials using more than 40% of global resources. It is responsible for around 50% of non-recyclable waste, up to 40% of the world's total carbon emissions, and it uses more than 35% of available energy [5]. If we now combine such data with the need to increase construction productivity for housing purposes, it is clear that current construction systems are not sustainable anymore, and the risk of facing a global ecological crisis is real and almost inevitable. For these reasons, reappraising existing construction methods and rethinking new sustainable construction methodologies represents a priority for the future of the built environment and – more in general – for the future of the entire planet.

Today, the mission for architecture on a global scale is addressing the current ecological crisis combining the full technological potential of computation and robotics with ethically-driven design creativity. Bob Sheil's words are particularly significant in this regard:

Running core to this mission is the capability to harness vast potential for precision measurement, complex modelling, and synthesised manufacturing, including machine learning and artificial intelligence, using
renewable materials, optimised and autonomous methods, with ethically-
minded and generous design creativity. [6]

Combining advanced technology and ethic inside a contemporary operative architecture may conduct to countless benefits for the construction industry. Inside an industrial sector historically reluctant to any technological advancement—in this regard, it is worth highlighting the fact that
the construction industry is currently the industrial sector with the lo-
west degree of digitisation [7]—the combination of computation and robotics with sustainability can represent the most appropriate operative
approach for the rise of a resilient architecture able to develop the built
environment towards a more feasible and sustainable future.

Advanced sustainability in design and construction

Today, the main ecological challenges for architecture and the construction industry are diminishing resources and the carbon footprint of building construction. A pertinent approach to face such issues—and at the
same time providing the required amount of buildings—is the so-called
"building more with less," namely building lighter and cheaper, optimising
structural and environmental performances, developing fabrication processes based on smart production and assembly procedures. Such a target
can be achieved through the employment of advanced technologies related to computational methods and robotic fabrication. Leaving to the following paragraph further explanations related to the use of robotics in
building design and construction, the focus of the current paragraph is
on computational methods. In this regard, there are three main applications where the use of computation is able to produce significant benefits
in terms of sustainability: environmental computation, structural optimisation and material performance.

In terms of environmental computation, there is an increasing trend inside the architectural discipline to set design workflows for the simulation of sustainable models. As explained by Brady Peters and Terry Peters
in their book *Computing the Environment. Digital Design Tools for Simulation and Visualisation of Sustainable Architecture* [8], such workflows are promoting the use of new computational tools able to optimise design solutions according to a multitude of factors such as internal comfort, energy
efficiency and CO_2 emissions. Such optimisation refers to several parameters, such as daylight, thermal exposure, airflow, turbulence, wind, space

syntax, and traffic flow. Although the consideration of these parameters and the use of sophisticated computational techniques might suggest a more technical engineering approach to architectural design, an optimistic point of view to sustainable design can produce an independent architectural language in which buildings are shaped by environmental forces combined with parametric and generative design procedures. There are several examples—related to both academic and professional environments—to highlight such emerging methodologies in architecture. For instance, CompSustNet (Computational Sustainability Network) is a research network sponsored by the American National Science Foundation, which gathers thirteen U.S. academic institutions led by Cornell University, and in particular the Institute for Computational Sustainability. Moreover, the work of specialist groups of environmental consultants inside existing architectural offices represents an essential reference for design and construction innovation based on more sustainable approaches. For example, BIG Ides is a team of environmental consultants at BIG (Bjarke Ingels Group), which combines expertise in design, computation and performance simulation to develop custom computational tools able to generate design solution concerning social and environmental conditions [9].

Regarding structural optimisation, there is a long history of research starting from Antoni Gaudí and its models of curved catenary forms, continuing with Frei Otto and his form-finding techniques, and now through computational-led research [10]. In terms of sustainability, it is interesting to highlight the fact that the use of structural optimisation technologies is strictly related to the optimised use of traditional construction materials. For instance, considering concrete construction represents a significant example in this regard since cement alone is a contributor to around 8% of the world's carbon dioxide emissions, representing a significant source of greenhouse gas production. Reducing material consumption through structural optimisation is a fundamental aspect in concrete construction, and numerous studies have highlighted the fact that there are wide margins for increasing the performance of current structural design methodologies and at the same time reaching possible reductions of up to 70% of the final volume of concrete[11]. An interesting example moving towards the realisation of optimised concrete structures is represented by *Stereoform Slab*, a research project developed by the collaboration between Odico, SOM and James McHugh Construction. Presented as a full-scale prototype at the 2019 Chicago Architecture Biennial, the project explores the use of low-cost EPS formwork production through robotic wire-cutting technologies pursuing the purpose of reducing carbon emissions due to the construction of concrete floor slabs, which generally represent around 40 to 60% of the total carbon emissions generated by standard projects. Regarding the particular case of Stereoform Slab, the use of structural optimisation procedures allows an extension of the concrete span up to 50%,

a reduction of 14% in total flexural steel reinforcing, and a total carbon reduction of approximately 20% [12].

The last application related to the combination of computation and sustainability is material performance. Regarding material science, research
in terms of sustainability can be conducted according to two approaches:
the first one considering traditional construction materials and the second one experimenting new construction materials. While the experimentation on new constuction materials will be further discussed in the
following paragraph talking about bio-materiality and additive methodologies for automated procedures, it is interesting to highlight the fact that
there are traditional construction materials which can be highly suitable for the production of sustainable construction processes. Sustainability in materials means: using local products and promoting regional as op-
posed to transcontinental production and transport; ensuring the source
of material at low-cost and from renewable resources; planning for an easy waste recovery; aiming to low-energy fabrication processes to achieve
a small environmental footprint in production; taking advantages of embedded material properties avoiding material transformation through the
use of chemical additives. According to such points, clay construction and
timber construction represent the more promising construction typologies in pursuing a productive and sustainable future for the construction
industry through the use of traditional materials.

Although several research projects are trying to extend clay construction
methodologies towards more efficient approaches using additive manufacturing and robotic fabrication [13], the research conducted on timber construction by the new Cluster of Excellence IntCDC (Integrative Computational Design and Construction for Architecture) at the University of Stuttgart
represents a paramount reference in advanced material performance. In
particular, two of the recent projects realised by the Cluster—the *BUGA
Wood Pavilion* [14] and the *Urbach Tower* [15]—show how advanced computational technologies and robotic fabrication can be combined inside a design and construction framework able to obtain the highest structural performance possible using the minimal amount of material. For instance, the
BUGA Wood Pavilion's 30m span covers an area of 500m^2 using only 45m^3 of
wood. At the same time, the *Urbach Tower* minimises the use of energy and
labour during fabrication processes by using the inner capacities of timber
to self-shaping itself according to oriented material programming routine.
In this particular case, such routine consists of a forming process based on
loss of wood moisture which allows for a self-shaping manufacturing process for high curvature CTL structures. In doing so, both structural performance and material synthesis allow an optimised construction process able
to use resources in a highly efficient way and to give life to genuinely sustainable architecture and construction processes.

Robotic fabrication in architecture

The use of timber construction as a suitable constructive approach for a more sustainable built environment implies a vast use of robotic fabrication methodologies, such as additive assembly, subtractive fabrication, automated large-scale spatial assembly. This consideration leads the research of this paper into the more specific realm of robotic fabrication in architecture, and further clarifications are required to understand the full potential of a sustainable approach for robotics inside the construction industry.

Although the first industrial robot was created by the American inventor George Charles Devol in 1954—the robotic system was called Unimate (Programmed Article Transfer)—architects started to explore the use of automated systems only from the 1990s, but the connection between building systems and automation systems where mainly based on a strict dependency of the former to the latter. Such trend remained in place until the beginning of the 21st century when the first industrial robotic fabrication laboratory for non-standard architectural fabrication processes was installed at the ETH Zurich in 2005, and robotic fabrication entered the architectural mainstream thanks to pioneering design researchers who used automated procedures to address issues related to topics like structural performance and architectural language. In doing so, a more integrated approach between building systems and automation systems arose, and today the relationship between such systems is moving towards a more comprehensive integrative co-evolution where both building systems and automation systems are employed according to multiple tasks rather than be strictly project-oriented.

Nowadays, robotic fabrication is rapidly spreading across a wide range of industrial sectors. According to PwC, 59% of manufactures already use robotics [16], and this number is expected to increase even more as the price of robots decreases and more functionality becomes available. In addition to that, IDC (International Data Corporation) highlights significant growth in worldwide spending on robotics and related services, setting a compound annual growth rate of 17% [17]. Such global trend is hitting the construction industry as well, and robots are starting to be used in several stages of the architectural process, such as the design and simulation of new computational approaches using neural networks and machine learning algorithmic procedures; experimentations with novel materials and material processes such as time-based bio-material deposition or digitally controlled concrete injection; structural optimisation processes such as bespoke concrete reinforcement and formworks; highly-versatile wood processing for complex timber structure; advanced hybrid subtractive-additive 3D printing procedures.

Among such a broad spectrum of uses and methodologies, it is interesting to note that all of them have one main thing in common, that is the technologically advanced sustainable approach that they can bring inside the construction industry. Robots can make manufacturing more sustainable in lots of different ways. For instance, robotic fabrication can significantly help in reducing waste and saving energy—in the order of up to 30% by optimising manufacturing processes [18]—allowing for more efficient off-site material production processes or eliminating dangerous on-site construction jobs. Furthermore, robots can deliver high-quality products based on consistent and predictable simulation models. Although there are several advantages in employing robotics during construction processes, the use of robots in construction still presents several limitations. For instance, the working environment continually changes during the building process, and such working conditions are quite challenging for automated processes. Furthermore, most of the buildings are unique, and their construction requires a high level of on-site mobility. Finally, the accuracy of robots is very high, while the accuracy on the building site is much lower. For these reasons, several types of research are currently conducted inside the most important institutions and universities around the world as a global attempt to make robotics more efficient for construction applications.

There are several methodologies to apply robotic fabrication inside a construction framework. The most important of them are additive manufacturing, subtractive fabrication, and automated spatial assembly. From a perspective of ecology and sustainability, it is interesting to note that such primary methodologies are currently developed towards more sustainable approaches. For instance, additive manufacturing is employing new bio-materials, while timber construction represents the primary building system to orient subtractive fabrication towards more ecological and carbon-free construction. In addition to that, in terms of automated spatial assembly, new sustainable methods are developed according to several approaches, such as mixed reality craftmanship through neural networks and machine learning or mobile multi-robot systems. For these reasons, further examples are required to understand better the current trend in the construction industry to combine robotic fabrication and sustainability inside a practical framework.

Regarding additive manufacturing, the most significant developments in terms of sustainability are related to the use of new materials. In general, accessible materials for 3D printing—especially those used for rapid prototyping—are derived from petroleum products such as thermoset and thermoplastic polymers. Not all plastics, however, are equal from the sustainability point of view, as thermoplastics such as ABS can be recycled and PLA is compostable in controlled environments. An example combining the use of PLA and robotic fabrication is represented by *Voxel Chair 1.0*, a prototype chair developed for robotic 3D printing by Manuel Jimenez Garcia, Gilles Retsin and Vicente Soler at the Design Computational Lab at The Bartlett School of Architecture, UCL [19]. The chair was generated from a 2.36km long toolpath assembled into one continuous line, and it was printed with a pellet extruder using PLA raw plastic particles rather than a filament. Always regarding the employment of new materials in design and construction, recent research in terms of material sustainability are moving towards the so-called "bio-materiality", which is a combination of biology, material science, ecology for a biologically-led architecture with a zero-net-carbon footprint. An example of such an approach is represented by the project *Cellusonic Biocomposites for Sustainable Manufacturing* developed by the Singapore University of Technology and Design [20]. In this case, the use of biological polymers produced by plants and animals allows creating a family of lightweight bio-composites construction material—called FLAM (Fungal-Like Adhesive Materials)—which can be employed for the construction of structure fully embedded within ecological cycles for a fundamentally sustainable approach to manufacturing.

In terms of subtractive fabrication, one of the most important use in terms of sustainability is the optimisation of cutting technologies which allow reducing both material waste and material use significantly. Regarding material waste, timber construction is a particularly suitable case study since the construction of timber components is generally related to cutting procedures where there is a consistent amount of material waste—although most of the time, timber can be recycled and addressed for other purposes. In terms of material use, an efficient cutting strategy may allow producing formworks to cast concrete structure, saving a significant amount of material. In general, such strategies run in parallel to topological optimisation procedures, which allow reducing the use of concrete, targeting specific structural requirements. For instance, research conducted at the Graz University of Technologies regarding additive fabrication for concrete elements allow the creation of concrete slabs using on average at least 30-40% less material with the possibility to increase such number up to 70% if shell effects are also used [21].

Finally, automated spatial assembly represents one of the most innovative fields of research in contemporary robotic fabrication applied to construction. New approaches such as mixed reality craftmanship through neural networks and machine learning or mobile multi-robot systems are making robotic automation more flexible and adaptable to the changing working conditions related to the nature of labour inside the construction industry. In addition to that, if we consider the increasing research on in-site robotic fabrication methodologies—something already started in 2011 by Fabio Gramazio and Matthias Kohler at the ETH Zurich [22]—it is possible to highlight a global effort in making robotics more flexible and able to adapt to changeable conditions.

In terms of mobile multi-robot systems, they are based on the opportunity to use sensor technology to open up robotic fabrication to new applications. In fact, with sensor technologies, robots can identify and locate objects, adapt robotic paths to product dimensions, and adjust process parameters to changeable requirements. An interesting example regarding such matter is the concept of deploying collaborative heterogeneous robotic systems developed by Maria Yablonina and Achim Menges at the ICD (Institute for Computational Design and Construction) at the University of Stuttgart [23]. The research project deploys smaller robots for the construction of a lightweight structure made of filament materials. Multiple task-specific machines are designed to manipulate and pass filament materials in an on-site internal architectural environment. In doing so, the limitations represented by existing on-site robotic strategies are expanded towards more flexible and adjustable design configurations and fabrication methods.

Another relevant field of development in terms of automated spatial assembly is the application of robotic fabrication procedures related to mixed reality craftsmanship. Regarding this approach, new robotic systems can be developed combining standard robotic fabrication with different sensing strategies and machine learning techniques for further application in the realm of design to manufacturing workflow. For instance, the research project developed by Giulio Brugnaro and Sean Hanna at The Bartlett School of Architecture (UCL) on adaptive robotic training methods for subtractive manufacturing is of particular significance in this regard [24]. The project develops a method to train an adaptive robotic system for subtractive manufacturing with timber. Such a method is based on a procedure involving sensor feedback, machine learning and material exploration. The intention is to experiment with a non-standard fabrication procedure resembling traditional craftmanship and considering heterogeneous material properties for a more adaptable automation process. In doing so, the trained networks successfully predict fabrication parameters demonstrating the opportunity to include human knowledge and material heterogeneity in robotic systems.

The socio-cultural implications of robotics

Until now, the discussion has been conducted about how advanced computational methods and robotic fabrication procedures can effectively lead to a more sustainable future for the built environment. Although the use of advanced technology in construction represents a positive aspect in many ways, there are several social and cultural implications about the use of robotics in the construction industry which need to be considered for a more comprehensive understanding of robotics in construction. In fact, inside an industry which employs around 7% of the world population, many people argue that such new robotic evolution of the built environment may lead to obsolescence of human labour, and therefore there is a real possibility to face a deep unemployment crisis. In reality, as already well pointed out by Henriette Bier, "the question is not whether but how robotic systems can be incorporated into building processes and buildings" [25] since the process is already started and most likely very difficult to interrupt. For this reason, it is more appropriate to conduct further observations about the socio-cultural implications of robotic fabrication rather than merely being reluctant or sceptical about something which is going to be inevitable.

In terms of socio-cultural implications related to the use of robotic fabrication inside the construction industry, it is fundamental to understand that such use has led to an entirely new epistemology of collective making that is creative in itself and inevitably oriented to the future. Regarding such matter, it is interesting to note that if the first robotic age—the age of industrial automation—vastly improved our physical productivity, the second robotic age—the ongoing one—is distinguishing itself as a driver of creative capacity. The advancements in computation and automation systems are making robots able to develop new intentional levels of creativity, creative resources only possible through unprecedented levels of complexity and novelty nested inside the development of computation and robotic procedures. To exemplify the rise of new emergent creativity and changes in terms of physical productivity, it is essential to take into account how robotics are affecting the two main subjects interested in such evolution of the built environment, namely architecture and the human being.

In regards to architecture, as robotics becomes increasingly commonplace, the subject of the debate can no longer be the dematerialisation of it into pure form—the way was happening during the 1990s—but the need for new resilient architecture is opening up the prospect of an entirely new aesthetic that could fundamentally alter the architectural design and the building culture. A similar implication has been pointed out by Mollie Claypool, Manuel Jimenez Garcia, Gilles Retsin, and Vicente Soler in their book *Robotic Building. Architecture in the Age of Automation* [26] highlighting the fact that the development of computational technologies and robotic fabrication in architecture is not only giving life to new forms of production and manufacturing but, first and foremost, is generating new methods of design thinking. The reason for it is that the entire design framework can move towards an automated robotic assembly rather than customised design decisions dictated by the human designer. In doing so, moving the point of view from the customisation of parts to the customisation of assembly leads architecture towards an entirely new realm, "a move towards a non-geometrical, data-based architecture that consists only of parts and their relationship" [26: 62]. As a consequence, it is possible to create an architecture where there is no distinction between elements—for instance, structure equal to cladding, columns equal to floors—and therefore, a new architectural order based on totalitarian parataxis might be realistically possible.

Whether the future of architecture will be based on a new paratactic order or not, the objective point of what has been said so far is the fact that the frenetic implementation of robotic fabrication processes inside the construction industry is practically forcing architecture's arrival in the digital age. However, the theoretical implications and future prospects of such arrival remain still vague, especially if considering them through the lens of architectural history. Learning from history implies a series of points of awareness, and one of them consists of being aware of the fact that any technological development is a matter of human progress; therefore, a comprehensive evolution is not possible without looking at the reality in a holistic and epistemological way. For this reason, explorations into robotic construction must be both practical and theoretical, namely referring to the robot not only as a medium of production but also as an epistemological point of view able to entirely influence production systems and the measure of human labour adopted by them.

In terms of the human being and the role of human labour in a built environment characterised by robotics, Antoine Picon's words are particularly significant:
    The human workforce seems to be so far missing from this narrative, as if an exclusive dialogue between designers and robots were the only development worth exploring. [...] Designers tend to occupy the place formerly devoted to craftsmen, that of inspired artisans shaping the world with their hands – digitally augmented hands that is. [27]

It is legitimate to think that in robotic fabrication, the role devoted to the workforce is generally minimised. In a similar way, it is also legitimate to think that if future buildings are constructed using technologies such as 3D printing and robotics, the industry will require either new highly skilled digital talents to migrate to that sector or an increase in the skills of existing workers to use software and programming applications necessary to manage such new technologies. In other words, even though there might be a reduction of the demand for traditional human labour, such reduction might be compensated by a new qualitative shift of human labour itself towards more advanced and safe tasks. In fact, from one side, robots could be employed in dangerous tasks saving human beings from being involved in high-risk jobs, while from the other side, human beings can be encouraged to develop more advanced computational skills to control complicated tasks in a more efficient way. In both cases, the step to make is imagining a new unified design and fabrication model based on constant interaction between designers and workers from one side, and computers and robots from the other.

Conclusion: how green robots can be

Several observations have been made and discussed during the paper, most of them referring to the current relationship between sustainability and robotic fabrication inside the construction industry. This relationship relies on constant interactions between human and non-human or cyber-physical agents, not only at design and production stages but also from the building operation side, where users and environmental conditions contribute to the emergence of various architectural configurations. As said before, the question is not if it is better to use robotic systems or not, but how to integrate them into building design and construction: the future of construction will be based on computational technologies and robotic fabrication, and they will inevitably influence architecture.

The main issue for architects is how to integrate such new technologies in a progressive idea of architecture. To achieve this target, architects must first stop being mere craftsmen, and they should start to understand the current digital evolution of architecture as a whole epistemological problem. The ongoing tendency of reducing the architect's action to compartmented tasks is significantly contributing to the loss of the ability to read the surrounding reality critically. Such loss leads to the result of producing a significant amount of research which most of the time is fragmented and unable to fit into a holistic view for the future of architecture. Secondly, architects need to expand such a new holistic view of digital opportunities towards more sustainable construction methods. In this regard, things like using new sustainable materials, optimising the use of traditional materials to reduce carbon footprint during material production and on-site construction, improving efficiency, flexibility and safety during construction processes and assembly, all these aspects are parts of a new approach and sensibility towards design and construction issues. The new approach and sensibility are going to constitute paramount factors for the future of architecture since one of the most urgent matters for contemporary architecture is to find an appropriate balance between sustainability and poetics for the rise of an efficient and aesthetically driven operative architecture.

There are several examples that can be taken into consideration as references for the construction of genuinely sustainable and robotic architecture; some of them have been already explained in the paper, and others can be considered moving forward. For instance, the project DFAB HOUSE developed by ETH Zurich within the Swiss National Centre of Competence in Research (NCCR) Digital Fabrication [28] represents a clear example of the full range of opportunities related to the use of digital fabrication in architecture. DFAB HOUSE is an architectural project to experiment and learn about the possibilities offered by digital architecture in a real-world setting, a sort of multi-technological digital fabrication applied to architecture, engineering and construction. Taking into consideration three main challenges—design interaction, upscaling and execution—under a unique holistic process, DFAB HOUSE combines six new digital building technologies for the construction of innovative buildings: in-situ fabricator, mesh mould, smart dynamic casting, smart slab, spatial timber assembly and lightweight translucent facade. In doing so, the DFAB HOUSE represents a 1:1 scale prototype of a comprehensive and possible architectural proposal based on computational technologies and robotic fabrication, where the use of energy and material resources are optimised and human labour oriented towards more advanced skills and procedures.

In conclusion, today we are facing the rise of a new integrated co-evolution of architecture, engineering, and construction. Such evolution is based on computation and robotics, pursuing the idea of a possible and necessary sustainable future for the built environment. This future seems to represent the more appropriate scenario to develop the construction industry to the level of innovation required by contemporary problems and ambitions. Environmental changes and climatic issues might only be fully understood and oriented by computational methods and advanced automated systems: only in this way, we will be able to leave to future generations something which will deserve further discussions and considerations.

[1] Zemp, M., Huss, M., Thibert, E. and al., "Global glacier mass changes and their contributions to sea-level rise from 1961 to 2016", in *Nature* 568, 2019, 382-6.

[2] *2018 Revision of World Population Prospects*, Population Division of the Department of Economic and Social Affairs, United Nations Secretariat, 2018.

[3] Knippers, J., Sheil, R. and Ramsgaard Thomsen, M., "Innochain: A Template for Innovative Collaboration" in Sheil, B., Ramsgaard Thomsen, M., Tamke, M. and Hanna, S. (Eds.), *Design Transactions: Information Modelling for a New Material Age*, UCL Press, 2020, 14-21.

[4] Renz, A. and Solas, M., *Shaping the Future of Construction. A Breakthrough in Mindset and Technology*, Technical Report, World Economic Forum, 2016.

[5] UN Environment and International Energy Agency, *Towards a Zero-Emission, Efficient, and Resilient Buildings and Construction Sector. Global Status Report 2017*, 2017.

[6] Sheil, B., "From Making Digital Architecture to Making Resilient Architecture", in Burry, J., Sabin, J., Sheil, B. and Skavara, M. (Eds.), *Fabricate 2020*, UCL Press, 2020, 16.

[7] McKinsey Global Institute, *Reinventing Construction. A Route to Higher Productivity*, McKinsey & Co, February 2017.

[8] Peters, B. and Peters, T., *Computing the Environment. Digital Design Tools for Simulation and Visualization of Sustainable Architecture*, AD Smart 06, Wiley, 2018.

[9] Peters, B., "BIG Ideas: Information Driven Design", in Peters, B. and Peters, T., *Computing the Environment. Digital Design Tools for Simulation and Visualization of Sustainable Architecture*, AD Smart 06, Wiley, 2018, 150-62.

[10] Burry, M., "Antoni Gaudí and Frei Otto. Essential Precursors to the Parametricism Manifesto" in Schumacher, P. (Ed.), *Parametricism 2.0. Rethinking Architecture's Agenda for the 21st Century*, AD Profile 240 (March-April 2016), 30-5.

[11] Kulkarni, A. R. and Bhusare, M. V., "Structural Optimization of Reinforced Concrete Structures", in *International Journal of Engineering and Technical Research*, 5 (7), 123-7.

[12] Attraya, R., Becus, R., Devin, A., Rossi, G., Sondergaard, A. and Vansice, K., "A Factory on the Fly", in Burry, J., Sabin, J., Sheil, B. and Skavara, M. (Eds.), *Fabricate 2020*, UCL Press, 2020, 92-9.

[13] Cabay, E., Dubor, A., Izard, J., Markopoulou, A., Rodriguez, M. and Sollazzo, A., "On-Site Robotics for Sustainable Construction", in Block, P., Byrne, K., Hutter, M., Schork, T. and Willmann, J. (Eds.), *Robotic Fabrication in Architecture, Art and Design 2018*, Springer, 2018, 390-401; Real, R. and San Fratello, V., "Mud Frontiers", in Burry, J., Sabin, J., Sheil, B. and Skavara, M. (Eds.), *Fabricate 2020*, UCL Press, 2020, 22-7.

[14] Aldinger, L., Alvarez, M., Bechert, S., Groenewolt, A., Knippers, J., Menges, A., Krieg, O. D., Sonntag, D. and Wagner, H. J., "The BUGA Wood Pavilion – Integrative Interdisciplinary Advancements of Digital Timber Architecture", in *ACADIA 2019: Ubiquity and Autonomy*, Proceedings of the 39th Annual Conference of the Association for Computer Aided Design in Architecture (ACADIA), 490-9.

[15] Aldinger, L., Bechert, S., Burgert, I., Grönquist, P., Knippers, J., Lehmann, K., Menges, A., Riggenbach, D., Rüggeberg, M., and Wood, D., "From Machine Control to Material Programming. Shelf-Shaping Wood Manufacturing of a High Performance Curved CTL Structure – Urbach Tower", in Burry, J., Sabin, J., Sheil, B. and Skavara, M. (Eds.), *Fabricate 2020*, UCL Press, 2020, 50-7.

[16] PwC, *Robot-ready: Adapting a new generation of industrial robots*, June 2018. https://www.pwc.com/us/en/industries/industrial-products/library/industrial-robot-ready.html. Accessed 21 July 2020.

[17] Vanian, J., "The Multi-Billion Dollar Robotics Market is About to Boon", in *Fortune*, 24 February 2016. https://fortune.com/2016/02/24/robotics-market-multi-billion-boom/. Accessed 21 July 2020.

[18] WHEB, What Robot can do for Sustainability, November 2014. https://www.whebgroup.com/what-robots-can-do-for-sustainability/. Accessed 21 July 2020.

[19] Jimenez Garcia, M., Retsin, G. and Soler, V., "Voxel Chair 1.0", in Claypool, M., Jimenez Garcia, M., Retsin, G. and Soler, V., *Robotic Building. Architecture in the Age of Automation*, Edition Detail, 2019, 66-7.

[20] Dritsas, S., Fernandez, J. G., Halim, S., Sanandiya, N., Teo, R. and Vijay, Y., "Cellulosic Biocomposites for Sustainable Manufacturing", in Burry, J., Sabin, J., Sheil, B. and Skavara, M. (Eds.), *Fabricate 2020*, UCL Press, 2020, 74-81.

[21] Freytag, D., Hansemann, G., Holzinger, C., Huy Kim, H., Peters, S., Schmid, R., Sliskovic, V., Tapley, J. and Trummer, A., "Additive Fabrication of Concrete Elements by Robots", in Burry, J., Sabin, J., Sheil, B. and Skavara, M. (Eds.), *Fabricate 2020*, UCL Press, 2020, 124-9.

[22] Helm, V., "In-Situ Fabrication. Mobile Robotic Units on Construction Sites", in Gramazio, F. and Kohler, M. (Eds.), *Made by Robots: Challenging Architecture at a Larger Scale*, AD Profile 229 (May/June 2014), 100-7.

[23] Yablonina, M. and Menges, A., "Towards the Development of Fabrication Machine Species for Filament Materials", in Block, P., Byrne, K., Hutter, M., Schork, T. and Willmann, J. (Eds.), *Robotic Fabrication in Architecture, Art and Design 2018*, Springer, 2018, 152-66.

[24] Brugnaro, G. and Hanna, S., "Adaptive Robotic Training Methods for Subtractive Manufacturing", in *ACADIA 2017: Disciplines and Disruption*, Proceedings of the 37th Annual Conference of the Association for Computer Aided Design in Architecture (ACADIA), 164-69.

[25] Bier, H., Anton, A., Bodea, S., Liu Cheng, A. and Mostafavi, S., "Robotic Building as Integration of Design-to-Robotic-Production and -Operation", in Bier, H. (Ed.), *Robotic Building*, Springer, 2018.

[26] Claypool, M., Jimenez Garcia, M., Retsin, G. and Soler, V., *Robotic Building. Architecture in the Age of Automation*, Edition Detail, 2019.

[27] Picon, A., "Robots and Architecture. Experiments Fiction Epistemology", in Gramazio, F. and Kohler, M. (Eds.), *Made by Robots: Challenging Architecture at a Larger Scale*, AD Profile 229 (May/June 2014), 58.

[28] Apolinarska, A., Baur, M., Dorfler, K., Grazer, K., Hack, N., Hall, D., Jipa, A., Kohler, M., Lloret-Fritschi, E., Sandy, T. and Sanz Pont, D., "DFab House. A comprehensive demonstrator of digital fabrication in architecture", in Burry, J., Sabin, J., Sheil, B. and Skavara, M. (Eds.), *Fabricate 2020*, UCL Press, 2020, 130-9.

TEACHING ARCHITECTURE WITHOUT ARCHITECTS

Architectural Pedagogy in the Age of Digitisation

Unpublished

Keywords: *architecture, digitisation, education, interdisciplinarity, teaching.*

Introduction: architecture as a necessity in extinction

In 1964 Bernard Rudofsky organised the exhibition *Architecture Without Architects* at the Museum of Modern Art in New York [1]. The exhibition consists of a wide photographic selection of the so-called "non-pedigreed architecture," to better say all that part of vernacular and primitive architecture built by anonymous builders rather than well-known architects. Apart from the interest of the subject and the polemic position adopted by Rudofsky concerning the rise of the dominant style of his time—the International Style [2]—and its neglected ability to produce architecture as a carbon copy of empty capitalism, it is now interesting highlighting the fact that such exhibition represents a pivotal moment in the history of architecture, particularly in regards to the reconsideration of any orthodox position related to scientific development and technological positivism. A similar critical point of view—not in the contents, but in the attitude—seems now more appropriate than ever due to the frenetic increase of digital technologies inside the architectural discipline. Therefore, a critical reappraisal of the current digital evolution seems a necessary action

Abstract

This paper seeks to analyse the relationship between architecture and education in the current age of digitisation, prefiguring a possible perspective for the rise of a new approach to architectural pedagogy.

During the last thirty years, the use of computational technologies related to architecture has exponentially increased. From an educational perspective, such an aspect has given life to new academic courses based on a new transdisciplinary understanding of the architectural problem. As a consequence of this development, new forms of architecture are arising, and an entirely new generation of architects is educated inside a new scientific background of knowledge. Students are exposed to a broader spectrum of ideas and methods where architecture stops being the centre of the studies, becoming one part of a far more complex system.

The evidence suggests that the increasing use of digital technologies and the introduction of disciplines related to the new digital reality are giving life to new forms of education and methods of research where the role of teachers and students is mixed together according to a new paratactic approach dictated by the rise of digital interdisciplinarity. In such a background of continuous evolution, what is the future of architecture and its education? Will the future of architecture be written by architects, or we will witness the rise of a new architecture without architects?

to undertake for a better understanding of the present and the future of architecture.

As explained by Kostas Terzidis through his construction of a new "algotecture", there is an increasing use of algorithmic design inside the architectural discipline [3]. Nowadays, the use of computational technologies and data analysis is significantly changing the identity of architecture, and the role of the architect during its conception and realization. Among a series of fields that can be taken into consideration to understand the measure of such change, robotic fabrication represents a significant example of the fact that the development of computational technologies in architecture is not only giving life to new forms of production and manufacturing but first and foremost is generating new methods of design thinking. As explained by Mollie Claypool, Manuel Jimenez Garcia, Gilles Retsin, and Vicente Soler in their book *Robotic Building. Architecture in the Age of Automation* [4], focusing on automation and robotic fabrication implies the fact that there is no need to invent a design solution since design decisions can be taken in real-time thanks to computational processes emerging from the combination and interaction between robots. In doing so, the entire design framework can move towards an automated robotic assembly rather than customised design decision dictated by the human designer. Moving the point of view from the customisation of parts to the customisation of assembly leads architecture towards an entirely new realm, "a move towards a non-geometrical, data-based architecture that consists only of parts and their relationship" [4: 62]. As a consequence of it, it is possible to create an architecture where there is no distinction between elements—for instance, structure equal to cladding, columns equal to floors—and therefore, the debate for architecture itself might be realistically over. After all, if architecture can be reduced to a mere assembly of components, the computational procedure dictating the assembly itself becomes more important than any socio-political context or existing anthropological point of view, bringing architecture to a natural loss of adherence with the surrounding reality.

Although such a scenario might seem critical and provocative, the possibility of facing the rise of architecture completely anonymous compare to any existing social environment is a real scenario that has already been taken into consideration in the past. For instance, already fifty years ago, Giancarlo De Carlo was arguing about the fact that such a detachment from existing realities was going to lead architecture to a very likely extinction. His words are particularly significant in this regard:

Looking coldly at what is happening, it is possible to say that architecture no longer interests anyone. It does not interest clients since it does not solve their problems of investment and power efficiently and rapidly; it does not interest institutions since it produces symbols which are too feeble and faded compared to those ones produced by other sectors of more powerful and aggressive activities; it does not interest common people since it does not propose anything able to match their expectations. Therefore, since nobody cares anymore, architecture is condemned to rapid extinction. [5]

Then, the architecture might face a phenomenon of extinction, and the current digital development—and the anonymity brought by it—might likely constitute a fertile background for such a phenomenon. However, before accepting any loss of architecture, it is more appropriate to ask ourselves a couple of questions: if nobody cares about architecture and architecture is condemned to rapid extinction, why do we need to study architecture? Why do we need to research it? In other words, why do we need to teach architecture?

Professional dilution: the role of the digital architect

To understand why we need to teach architecture, it is crucial to understand what kind of professional we want to educate, and the context of reference in which this new professional will act. To appreciate the role of the architect in a digital context where the architecture itself seems to have lost any form of primacy, we need to look twenty years back, more precisely at the end of the 20th century where the building industry was fundamentally broken. As explained by Dennis Shelden in his article, *Entrepreneurial Practice: New Possibilities for a Reconfiguring Profession* [6], from the end of the 20th century, inefficiency and dysfunctions significantly hit building design and the construction industry. The rise of a new technological trend fragmented the entire industry, causing disruption in terms of risk aversion, low investments and low compensation for the architectural profession, traditionally oriented to resist any form of technological advancement.

In such a context of disruption and significant changes, a minority group of companies began to conduct experiments inside the new technological opportunities, abandoning the common strategy adopted by the majority of the practices which focused their effort on implementing traditional business models. From that moment, algorithmic design spread across the architectural discipline, giving life to new spin-off companies connected to the mother practice—such as Gehry Technologies, for instance, a spin-off company generated by Frank Gehry's office. While for the pioneers of this new integrated approach, the creation of computational tools to support the creative process was a way to reclaim authority and control over the outcomes, the use of new technologies for contemporary practices is a way to diversify their services, a procedure to integrate their work, a process to reinvent their professional role towards a more entrepreneurial identity. The reasons why such new forms of integrated offices and entrepreneurial attitude found a fertile land of development inside the architectural discipline are well described by Dennis Shelden:

> Architects create vast amounts of new intellectual property over the course of design—new concepts, inventions, and methods—and are perhaps uniquely positioned to holistically take on problems and opportunities identified in the broader culture of resources and finances, people and technologies, natural and artificial systems. [...] The next decades will be a period of radically accelerated disruption and change for the profession. The traditional fragmented models of practice will be dramatically rewritten by integrated or alternative ones. [6: 10-3]

The ability to "holistically take on problems" is a distinctive feature of architects. Ben van Berkel adopts a similar holistic approach to the profession in describing the new spin-off company UNSense created from his well-known architectural practice UNStudio. Van Berkel clearly states the idea that "the role of the architect needs to become more holistic. The architect needs to be a cultural entrepreneur: interested in business, but also with a genuine passion for culture" [7: 61]. This holistic idea of the architect as "cultural entrepreneur" seems to be the more appropriate starting point for the construction of a pertinent school of architecture in the current digital era, a useful result to pursue in educating new generations of architects, the horizon towards which orienting a new holistic approach to architecture: pertinent to the panoptic view of our time, against any excess of specialism and clusterisation of knowledge.

Architecture in transdisciplinarity

Pursuing the idea to educate new generations of architects to holistically be "cultural entrepreneur," the first step to make is understating what the current digital culture is and where it comes from. Living in the middle of the "Fourth Industrial Revolution" [8] means living in an age where the introduction of cyber-physical systems is supporting from one site a new post-Fordist economy of production based on the fragmentation of labour and processes, while from the other side it is favouring a new neoliberal idea of a society where the rise of digital technologies is leading towards a new "transparency society" [9] able to take advantages of an apparently unlimited individual freedom. In a society based on post-Fordism and Neoliberalism, the economy translates its nature into the model of "command economy" [10]—or to better say, from a mass-produced supply-and-demand economy to a mass-customised "command economy" where products are made everywhere, and anytime they are required—and the nature of labour faces a new Fordist revival. Although our era is based on post-Fordism, it is interesting to note that such a new post-Fordist framework is based on a genetic paradox, namely a model generated by the same reduction of human labour into specialised and cost-effective tasks. If, in the past, people were serving mass-standardised productions during the Fordist era, now they are serving mass-customised productions. The main difference between the first Fordism and this new Fordist revival is that the former pursues the cost-effectiveness of products, while for the latter, the main point is the cost-effectiveness of services.

The genetic paradox of post-Fordism affects our society across several industries, in particular the service industry. Architectural offices and the work of architects lies inside such industry, and interesting enough, it is possible to see such paradox affecting the profession. In fact, it is not inappropriate saying that when new architects enter the profession, they are subjected to a workflow where they are employed in specific and repetitive tasks—which sometimes remain the same even after years of work. Such aspect reflects the reduction of human labour into specialisation generated by the genetic paradox of the current post-Fordist model. The architectural profession lies precisely in the middle of this paradox, and this aspect represents a crucial factor in considering what nowadays architectural pedagogy should be. If the future of new generations of architects will be based on high levels of specialization and compartmentation of knowledge, what is the point in teaching architecture, a discipline which is by nature based on a holistic cultural approach? Architecture can never be a matter of specialism as it involves too many areas—from technology and science to history, art and law.

To answer this question, it is important to understand the nature of the subjects acting inside the current educational framework—namely teachers and students—but this will be clarified later in the paper. For now, it is more appropriate to start with some consideration about the situation of architectural pedagogy in the current age of digitisation.

The current situation of architectural education represents a very complex universe composed of a significant range of courses and programmes. The most important institutions and universities around the world offer countless opportunities to continuously undertake academic studies, not only in terms of diversification of contents but also in terms of duration and delivery methods. For instance, short online courses based on new forms of smart-teaching are now giving the opportunity to quickly obtain certificates to develop skills related to both academic and professional environment. Such a new pedagogical abundance is not a coincidence if we consider it throughout the vocation of the current digital era intrinsically based on constant specialisation and clusterisation of knowledge, a time where the frenetic speed of evolution of digital technologies requires continuous improvement of personal skills. Such frenetic specialisation generates a series of collateral effects, and one of them is a consistent increase of the global academic offer; in other words, a bulimic need of knowledge potentially leading to everywhere and nowhere.

Considering the rise of this new pedagogical jungle deeply unappropriated to pursue the idea of educating new generations of architects to become "cultural entrepreneur," there is another way of teaching architecture which is arising inside the most important institutions and universities: the transdisciplinary approach. Talking about the transdisciplinary approach in architecture means highlighting a complex and ongoing process of renovation of the architectural discipline based on a constant collaboration with other disciplines—such as anthropology, sociology but also computer science, engineering, and management. The final result of this transdisciplinary approach is the creation of pedagogical methods in which architecture represents only one part of a far more complex system of knowledge that configures itself as a polycentric system, a sum of multiple focal points based on a paratactic order.

Among a series of possible references which can be discussed to support the appropriateness of such a transdisciplinary approach, a prominent example is represented by The Bartlett (UCL) and its new campus at Here East in London. With its fourteen departments—divided into schools, centres and institutes—The Bartlett represents one of the leading universities in the world for architectural studies. The departments embrace several disciplines spanning from architecture and engineering to computer science, business management, economy, and social politics. All of them collaborate to create a unique research environment able to educate students to the complexity and multiplicity of their future profession. The primary example of such a transdisciplinary approach is the new tech campus built at Here East in London. Inside one of the most vibrant technological hubs in Europe—obtained by the reuse of buildings forming part of the Olympic Park in 2012—the new campus is conceived as a unique space where both educational and productive activities are gathered under the same roof. The resulting open space is a unique place where students, teachers and professionals can learn and collaborate in experimenting with new materials, developing new methods and processes; in other words, an extraordinary welding bay where knowledge comes together in a pedagogical— and at the same time productive—way. Here East is the "London's home for making," and in this home, The Bartlett is experimenting with a new method of architectural pedagogy, a new transdisciplinary approach where a multitude of disciplines are gathered inside the same space, and students are constantly exposed to the complexity of their present.

There are other examples in contemporary architectural pedagogy where a similar transdisciplinary approach can be successfully identified. Other important universities are adopting pedagogical methods to promote interaction and collaboration across several departments combining a broad spectrum of disciplines and knowledge. The most important thing is now to highlight the fact that the same transdisciplinary organization of these universities is reflected in the educational offer provided to students. This approach seems to be the most appropriate one to adopt in the current digital era; the most appropriate model able to educate new generations of architects to be "cultural entrepreneurs" inside the complex reality represented by the current digital evolution of the built environment.

Learning from history the measure of our present

What has been said so far gives evidence to one simple but fundamental idea: according to the current status of our society, architecture cannot be considered a confined discipline anymore. As previously mentioned, the rise of the new Neoliberal dimension of our society and the fall of what Foucault would have called "disciplinary society" [11] leads towards an interdisciplinary world where architecture stops being the exclusive centre of architects' action and becomes one part of a far more complex system of knowledge. Although it has been said that interdisciplinarity is propaedeutic to the formation of an appropriate pedagogical model, the risk of losing architecture in such a vast background is real and might be a tangible possibility. For this reason, a quick look into the past may suggest some pertinent interpretative key through which understanding such a new extended horizon.

Architecture has never been taught as a singular discipline—at least not inside the most valuable schools of architecture—but it has always been placed inside a far more complex system of knowledge. Even the famous "design by dictation" promoted by the Beaux-Arts pedagogy—which has constituted the foundation of many contemporary universities, especially in the United States—was based on the combination of several arts – such as painting and sculpturing—but it was also legitimated by a deep understanding of the naturalistic positivism underneath the concept of Classicism and the use of classical elements inside a well-defined architectural composition. Such approach has progressively been replaced by the advent of more scientific positivism able to take over the classical reference to nature with a renovated use of the reason—the so-called Rationalism. In the cradle of the shift from Classicism to Rationalism, at the beginning of the 20th century, a new approach to architectural pedagogy was introduced at the Bauhaus. From it, a series of successive teaching experiences found in the Bauhaus the appropriate reference for the formulation of new educational models. Among them, two cases are particularly significant according to the analysis conducted through this paper: The Cooper Union directed by John Hejduk, and the Architectural Association directed by Alvin Boyarsky. Together with the Bauhaus directed by Walter Gropius, these three moments in the history of architectural pedagogy represent the best examples to define the measure of a contemporary interdisciplinary approach to architectural education. For this reason, what are the main teachings that it is possible to learn from them?

First of all, the Bauhaus. Founded in 1919 by Walter Gropius in Weimar, the Bauhaus considers architecture as a social art, or to better say, a unitary form of art able to condense realism and idealism inside the shape of new modern society. Walter Gropius clarifies many aspects related to the Bauhaus in his seminal book *Scope of Total Architecture* [12], published in the United States in 1955 after the years spent as chairman of the Department of Architecture at the Harvard University. Inside the Bauhaus, the organisation of the educational offer in "craft laboratories"—such as ceramics, weaving, metalworks—and the level of the academic staff—among the professors there were names such as Lyonel Feininger, Vasilij Kandinskij, Paul Klee, László Moholy-Nagy, and Oskar Schlemmer—give life to a unique educational experience in the history of architecture. Interesting enough, although one of the primary teaching purposes was architecture, no courses related to architecture were provided to students—at least not until 1927 when Gropius decided to start a new specific section of architecture, giving its control to the Swiss architect Hannes Mayer. For Gropius, theoretical studies specifically focused on architecture had to start not before the third year to keep the student's mind away from any form of historical imitation and intimidation.

The experience of the Bauhaus directed by Walter Gropius teaches us that it is not impossible to teach architecture without architects: it has already been done, and it has been one of the most successful models in architectural history. Teaching architecture without architects is neither a provocation nor a sentence to follow literally. It merely means that architects do not have to limit themselves inside a traditional and conservative understanding of their discipline. They have to open up their field of action and being able to consciously pass down to students a new extended system of knowledge: in other words, architects need to stop being only architects; they need to be cultural researchers actively engaged in the contemporary evolution of their time.

Another essential historical example in terms of architectural pedagogy is The Cooper Union directed by John Hejduk from 1975 to 2000. During his teaching experience already started in 1964, John Hejduk experiments the "education of an architect" [13] as nobody before, revolutionising the entire educational approach of the school and introducing a series of remarkable teaching methods and models—such as The Cube Problem, The Juan Gris Problem, Nine Square Grid Problem and Architectonics. The Cooper Union directed by Hejduk was based on "team-teaching", namely an interdisciplinary work characterised by a constant collaboration between professionals coming from different disciplines. Hejduk was able to gather inside the school painters, sculptures, poets, writers, acting according to a managerial role similar to what Walter Gropius did during his direction of the Bauhaus. Once again, the architect is the director of a complex system of knowledge: his task is not only to teach architecture, but most importantly, serving and leading among several different disciplines and professionals.

Finally, the last historical example in terms of architectural pedagogy is the Architectural Association directed by Alvin Boyarsky from 1971 to 1990. Alvin Boyarsky is a pivotal figure in the history of the Architectural Association, a school founded by students for students. Through his entrepreneurial ability, Boyarsky played a crucial role in saving the school from its closure at the end of the 1960s. At that time, the number of debts was forcing the school to lose its original independence in favour of the academic incorporation to the Imperial College and its more traditional way of teaching architecture. Through his creative eclecticism and a programme composed of a variety of courses and subjects—once again, similarities with the Bauhaus directed by Walter Gropius can be seen—Boyarsky organises the new pedagogical model of the Architectural Association around three main areas—general studies, technical studies and the Unit system—and an unconditional openness to any research proposed by students. Students were put at the centre of their studies which were oriented according to their interests. Such attitude—together with a continuous renovation of the teaching staff—allowed the school to keep untouched its experimental identity and guaranteed a prosperous heterogeneity of research and multiple regenerations of the architectural thinking. It is not a coincidence that some of the most influential architects of the second half of the 20th century found in the Architectural Association directed by Alvin Boyarsky the appropriate place to develop their research —such as Nigel Coates, Leon Krier, Charles Jencks, Bernard Tschumi, Rem Koolhaas and Zaha Hadid. Led by the same interdisciplinary approach characterising the Bauhaus directed by Walter Gropius and The Cooper Union directed by John Hejduk, the Architectural Association directed by Alvin Boyarsky represents a significant example of a school in which unconditional freedom and curiosity for knowledge allow to extend architecture far beyond its traditional disciplinary limits, giving it the chance to experiment the action of a transdisciplinary influence, discovering unexplored territories, breaking walls down and with them any prejudice or preclusion.

After having briefly analysed the Bauhaus directed by Walter Gropius, the Cooper Union directed by John Hejduk and the Architectural Association directed by Alvin Boyarsky, what is the most important lesson that it is possible to learn from them? These three moments in the history of architectural pedagogy show us the way for a pertinent interdisciplinary approach to architectural teaching, a method able to educate not only professionals but human beings, allowing them to serve and lead the world around them. The idea of "leading and serving" at the same time represents a crucial aspect concerning the architectural profession because a good architect has to serve others and at the same time being able to lead them: leading is not a matter of talent, it is based on a constant willingness to serve. Leading and serving are two indispensable factors to penetrate the surrounding reality critically, namely being able to look at it from a different point of perspective to reach a more focused understanding of its dynamics. As Mario Tronti explained almost sixty years ago, "within the society, and at the same time against it" [14]: this is the main point. Only in this way teaching and research conducted inside a school of architecture can educate new generations of architects to look into the surrounding reality as a comprehensive combination of human progress and technological development, in other words avoiding any sort of metamorphosis into automated specialists or encyclopaedic "know-it-alls."

The three schools of architecture analysed in this paragraph teach us that knowledge is made from a multitude of points of view, and it is far more complex and meaningful compare to any specialistic or encyclopaedic model. Knowledge is an active three-dimensional space continually evolving, and it is crucial to be curiously involved in the exploration of past and present realities and continuously being involved in the search for the future. Educating architects involves knowing architecture, and "there is no finality in architecture—only continuous change" [12: 70]. In the current digital era, such a "continuous change" is a distinctive feature of our society, and missing to understand the three-dimensional measure of knowledge means moving towards a new Fordist revival, namely reducing human work into specialised, simple tasks which lead to a far more significant discrepancy between the potential of technological means and the foresight of human intentions.

Teachers and students in the age of digitisation

The problem of the current architectural education reflects the problem of the evolution of the current digital society. Although referred to a past time, the words of Walter Gropius are particularly significant in this regard:
Our scientific age, by going to extremes of specialisation, has obviously prevented us from seeing our complicated life as an entity. The average professional man, driven to distraction by the multiplicity of problems spread out before him, seeks relief from the pressure of general responsibility in a specialised field and refuses to be answerable for anything that may happen outside this field. A general dissolution of context has set in and naturally resulted in shrinking and fragmenting life. As Albert Einstein once put it: "Perfection of means and confusion of aims seems to be characteristic of our age". [12: 142-3]

Following Gropius' ideas, the first step to make is to leave aside any specialism and to be focused on a comprehensive understanding of the architectural problem. Of course—as Gropius already highlights—the tendency of our time to move towards specialisation is well-rooted in the current society, and the reason for it is that specialisation supports a state of convenience: it is much easier taking only one responsibility rather than being involved in multitude problems at the same time. It is essential to understand that such a preference for convenience is not a coincidence, but once again, it is well-rooted inside the Neoliberal paradigm, which leads to the current evolution of our digital society. As explained by By-ung-Chul Han in his book *Psychopolitics: Neoliberalism and New Technologies of Power*:

Neoliberalism represents a highly efficient, indeed an intelligent, system for exploiting freedom. Everything that belongs to practices and expressive forms of liberty—emotion, play and communication—comes to be exploited. It is inefficient to exploit people against their will. Allow exploitation yields scant returns. Only when freedom is exploited are returns maximised. [15: 10]

The abuse of freedom highlighted in Byung-Chul Han's words is only one aspect belonging to a far more complex sociological and anthropological background characterising the current digital era. Among all the implications connected to it, it is clear that also architectural pedagogy is significantly changing in this evolving context. The point now is that this change is not only influencing teaching methods and models from a technical point of view, but such abuse of freedom is directly affecting the human subjects involved in the educational process, namely teachers and students.

In the age of digitisation, there is a clear paratactic tendency in the relationship between the teacher and the student. In continuation with an established tradition of architectural pedagogy for which "the teacher must not transmit knowledge and skills but need only to bring the student to discover a sort of key point within himself" [16], many of the current advanced courses in architecture allow students to pursue their research project according to their interests. Although such freedom is still very limited inside the majority of the more traditional architectural courses—especially for undergraduate studies where students need more specific guidance—the risk of the paratactic tendency in architectural education might constitute unintentional support to that abuse of freedom previously described referring to the Neoliberal construction of the current digital society. In other words, from one side, too little freedom for the student might lead to new forms of conservativism—coming from the teacher's background—while from the other side, too much freedom for the student might lead to new forms of limited research—coming from a lack of guidance and education. For this reason, what is an appropriate role of teachers and students for an effective architectural education? To answer this question, it is worth to quote Boyarsky's words:

The problem is to actually produce witty people who have got lots of conversations echoing in their ears, who have seen a lot, and who have met many people who are on their way up into the world. [17]

Therefore, the education of "witty people" is the primary purpose to pursue. To succeed in such a mission, both teachers and students need to act following the same conviction, that is considering the current digital evolution of architecture as a continuous dialogue between opposite variables, between technological specialisation and digital humanities. It is essential to look at the world around us with modesty and curiosity, being fully aware of the fact that to construct an operative architecture, it is crucial to look at the new digital reality not as mere technological development, but first and foremost as a matter of human progress. From one side, teachers need to educate students towards such understanding of the architectural problem. In contrast, students need to follow teachers without pursuing empty individualisms or being enchanted by the evolution of new digital tools and the passive social engagement promoted by them. "Being digital" [18] is, first of all, a matter of human condition, and only after genuinely understanding this point, technological advancements can be taken into consideration and developed with solid awareness. This aspect seems to be the most appropriate way to educate students referring to the current evolution of our digital society, to introduce them to the real reason of being an architect, something that was already well explained by Ernesto Nathan Rogers in one of his seminal articles published in *Casabella-Continuità* in the early '60s:

It is enough to know how to penetrate reality, extract its essences, establish immanent relationships, vivify such relationships and let them enter the evolutionary cycle of life so that they can mature and be carried out to encourage constantly new evolutionary changes. [19]

Conclusion: for a school of architecture

In the age of digitisation, evolutionary mutations happen on a daily basis. For this reason, the construction of a relevant architectural pedagogy has to promote a constant interaction with the surrounding reality and guarantee a critical penetration of it. This point seems the ultimate purpose of any pedagogical construction: being able to penetrate reality. It has been seen that in the architectural world, this means being able to connect a wide range of different disciplines due to the complex nature of the architectural problem itself. There is still the need to practically create an educational model able to address what it has been said so far correctly. Therefore, there is still a question that deserves an answer: how can a contemporary school of architecture be created?

To answer this question, two steps need to be made: firstly, there is need to decide what are the main disciplines currently affecting architecture; secondly, there is need to set the methods necessary to use in connecting such disciplines and leading them towards the construction of an operative architecture.

Regarding the main disciplines currently affecting architecture, they can be summarised in six actions which can be considered as containers of all the disciplines involved in a new architectural pedagogy in the age of digitisation: designing (product design, architectural design, urban design), engineering (structural engineering, material engineering), making (digital manufacturing, robotic fabrication), managing (economy, ecology, politics), programming (computer science, data analysis) and understanding (anthropology, sociology, cognitive science). Four of them—designing, making, programming and understanding—could be included in the first three years of studies purely based on learning, while the remaining two actions—engineering and managing—could constitute the main parts of the final two years, a time organised on a progressive move from learning towards proposing, namely from the first three years in which students—utterly new to the architectural discipline—may absorb a wide range of notions, to the final two years where the learning goal is shifted towards real dynamics of reality and professional context, giving to students the opportunity to put into practice what they have learnt in the previous three years, and—most importantly—developing their new ideas in a conscious and well-structured environment.

After having specified the main disciplines currently affecting architecture, the second step to make is setting the educational methods that we want to use in connecting such disciplines. In terms of pedagogical methods, merely looking at the history of architectural education provides a considerable number of examples to be inspired by. From the "craft laboratories" of the Bauhaus to the contemporary concept of "visiting schools" adopted by the Architectural Association, the examples are countless. In between, remarkable models and methods such as the "Architectonics" courses organised by John Hejduk at the Cooper Union or the "paperless studios" created by Greg Lynn at the Columbia University. In general, a faculty organised around the ideas of "team-teaching" and "visiting professors" might be the right combination of choices to organize the study plan over five years and to guarantee a continuous update of contents.

Furthermore, a study plan along five years allows offering a comprehensive understanding of the architectural problem, dividing the academic offer into two parts: the first three years of undergraduate studies and the final two years of postgraduate studies. Both parts might be organised around the combination of two methods: *teaching clusters* and *workshop series*. In the first three years of undergraduate studies, the teaching clusters would rotate around four of the main actions described above: designing, making, programming and understanding. These teaching clusters would constitute the majority of the academic studies, and they would be supported by semesterly workshop series where the students can practically consolidate what they learn inside the teaching clusters.

After these first three years, the last two would have the same division between teaching clusters and workshop series, but with two significant differences: firstly in terms of contents of the teaching clusters—now focused on managing and engineering rather than designing, making, programming and understanding—and secondly in terms of time balance between the two methods. If during the first three years the teaching clusters would constitute the majority of the studies, during the final two years the workshop series would progressively become the central part of them, perhaps even transforming themselves into professional series delivered by students themselves: in other words, becoming a first attempt to initiate students to the professional world.

In conclusion, these are only initial observations of a far more complex pedagogical project to teach architecture and to educate architects in the age of digitisation. The intent is to offer a comprehensive educational framework able to provide to students the necessary both practical and theoretical skills to serve and—at the same time—to lead the current digital evolution of our society. As said before, the crucial point is being able to penetrate the reality, be within it to be against it: in other words, learning the ability to adhere to the surrounding world while remaining detached from it, at least up to the point of being able to put it into a different perspective.

As Walter Gropius said more than sixty years ago, "our century has produced the expert type in millions; let us make way now for the men of vision" [12: 18]. If to reach such a purpose, there is the need to teach architecture without architects, it is still challenging to predict it with certainty at the current stage of our digital society, but one thing is for sure: architecture is a discipline base on a three-dimensional understanding of knowledge, a sort of knowledge in 3D full of interdisciplinarity. Therefore, the introduction in the architectural pedagogy of different disciplines and types of professionals is a fundamental point to provide a pertinent and appropriate education in the age of digitisation. A school of architecture is the centre of constant exchange and hybridization of knowledge, and—to pursue and to give life to such a belief—architects need to teach less and coordinate more. They need to stop being teachers of compartmented subjects and replacing such an attitude with the more comprehensive role of coordinators of studies, conscious ambassadors of evolutionary mutations always affecting the identity of architecture. In doing so, inside a future school of architecture, there will probably be less need for architects in terms of quantities, but certainly not in terms of quality, to guarantee a competent and forward-looking education. For this reason, probably in the future we will teach architecture with fewer architects, but certainly not without them.

[1] Rudofsky, B., *Architecture without Architects. A Short Introduction to Non-Pedigreed Architecture*, Museum of Modern Art, New York, 1964.

[2] Hitchcock, H. and Johnson, P., *The International Style: Architecture Since 1922*, Museum of Modern Art, New York, 1932.

[3] Terzidis, K., *Algorithmic Architecture*, Elsevier Architectural Press, 2006.

[4] Claypool, M., Jimenez Garcia, M., Retsin, G. and Soler, V., *Robotic Building. Architecture in the Age of Automation*, Edition Detail, 2019.

[5] De Carlo, G., "L'architettura della partecipazione" (1973), in Marini, S. (Ed.), *L'architettura della partecipazione*, Quodlibet, 2013, 76-7.

[6] Shelden, D., "Entrepreneurial Practice: New Possibilities for a Reconfiguring profession", in Shelden, D. (Ed.), *The Disruptors. Technology-Driven Architect-Entrepreneurs*, AD Profile 264 (March/April 2020), 6-13.

[7] Van Berkel, B., "The Role of Technologies within the Future of an Expanded Profession", in Shelden, D. (Ed.), *The Disruptors. Technology-Driven Architect-Entrepreneurs*, AD Profile 264 (March/April 2020), 58-65.

[8] Schwab, K., *The Fourth Industrial Revolution*, The Fourth Industrial Revolution, 2016.

[9] Han, B., *The Transparency Society*, Stanford University Press, 2015.

[10] Greenfield, A., *Radical Technologies: The Design of Everyday Life*, Verso Books, 2017, 89.

[11] Foucault, M., *La società disciplinare*, Vaccaro, S. (Ed.), Mimesis, 2010.

[12] Gropius, W., *Scope of Total Architecture*, Harper & Brothers, 1955.

[13] Hejduk, J., *Education of an Architect. The Irwin S. Chanin School of Architecture of the Cooper Union*, Rizzoli, 1989; and Hejduk, J., *Education of an Architect: a point of view. The Cooper Union School of Art and Architecture. 1964-1971*, The Monicelli Press, 1999.

[14] Tronti, M., *Operai e capitale*, Einaudi, 1966, 4.

[15] Han, B., *Psychopolitics: Neoliberalism and New Technologies of Power*, Verso Books, 2017.

[16] Brighenti, T., *Pedagogie architettoniche. Scuole, Didattica, Progetto*, Accademia University Press, 2018, 364.

[17] Sunwoo, I., "Pedagogy's Progress: Alvin Boyarsky's International Institute of Design", in *Grey Room*, n.34, 2009, 53.

[18] Negroponte, N., *Being Digital*, Alfred A. Knopf, 1995.

[19] Rogers, E. N., "Utopia della Realtà", in *Casabella-Continuità*, n.259, 1962.

ARCHITECTURE IN CONNECTOCRACY

Eight Digital Principles for an Operative Architecture

Unpublished

Keywords: *architecture, connectocracy, digitality, culture, society.*

Introduction: the paradoxical condition of being digital

Every historical period has its related language generated by the physical means of transmission and modelled by the mental interpretation of human beings. The change of language is directly proportional to the historical level of ongoing evolution, and the force of neologisms multiplies with the degree of innovation. In the contemporary digital discussion, terms like "cyborg," "cyberception," "cyberspace," [1] and "cyborculture" [2] are only some example of such ongoing change. In many cases, language has been transmitted thanks to technological advancements, and in recent years the electrification of language has led to the shift from an alphabet-centric world to another one based on an opposite electro-centric nature. The example of the suffix "cyber-" is just one case of a far more complex ongoing development, and it brings with it the sign of sociological and anthropological changes so significant and substantial to define the traits of an entirely new era.

Abstract

This paper seeks to define the concept of *connectocracy* and the rise of eight digital principles for the construction of an operative architecture. *Connectrocracy* is defined as the power of connectivity affecting the current evolution of the digital society, a socio-political, cultural, and anthropological system based on connectivity and virtual partnership promoted by digital technologies.

During the last thirty years, the use of digital technologies has produced significant changes in the evolution of contemporary society giving life to new forms of socio-political, cultural and anthropological modifications. The increasing virtual commitment of our daily life – promoted by the action of panoptic connectivity – has translated our society into its new digital realm.

The evidence suggests that in a time characterised by *connectocracy*, architecture needs new operative principles to be able to update its identity to the ongoing digital development. In such a new socio-political, cultural and anthropological background, what could a possible configuration for architecture be? What are the principles to use as critical concepts for the operative construction of a pertinent identity for architecture? Architecture is first and foremost a matter of social construction, and the analysis of the current *connectocratic society* represents an appropriate starting point for further research.

Focusing the attention on the ongoing changes of language in the current age of digitisation means reflecting the will of tracing a clear—although strictly interconnected—distinction between the first age of electricity—in other words, electrification—and the second age of electricity—the so-called digitisation. The main difference between the electrification of language and the digitisation of it lies in the different degree of mental penetration during the first and second age. If, in the first age of electricity, the TV-model represents the first degree of appropriation and detached command of the surrounding reality, the digital model makes possible a constant comparison and interaction with such reality in the second age of electricity. As a consequence of this change, the human being stops being an observer of the surrounding world to become a direct interlocutor of it. The shift from observer to interlocutor has made the human being increasingly dependent on new technological mediums, finding in them an instrument of legitimation.

Nowadays, we are becoming more dependent on our new level of virtual connectivity, and we feel a sense of frustration when we lose this connection even only for a few moments. Our dependence is so rooted in our new digital identity that we associate our very nature with that one obtained by the use of connective mediums, and we want them increasingly powerful to meet our new cyber-state. As explained by Marshall McLuhan, we are becoming more and more like Narcissus by elaborating his attitude in a technocratic way: as we are no longer able to observe ourselves, we spend our time looking at our digital alter ego, the "cyborg" who is within us. In such a new scenario, not only "the medium is the new message" [3] but— according to the current evolution of artificial intelligence through computation and robotics—the medium is almost becoming the new human being.

The fact that a new level of human "alienation"—speaking in Marx's terms—represents one of the main features inside the current "Fourth Industrial Revolution" [4] is a sign of the paradoxical condition affecting human life inside the current digital society. Such new digital reality is based on two socio-political and anthropological models, namely post-Fordism and Neoliberalism. From one side, a new post-Fordist economy of production based on the fragmentation of labour and processes is translating the focus of human specialisation from products to services, while from the other side, a new neoliberal idea of society is leading towards a new "transparency society" [5] able to take advantages of unlimited individual freedom. Byung-Chul Han has well explained the paradoxical condition of freedom in a Neoliberal society in his book *Psychopolitics: Neoliberalism and New Technologies of Power*:

Neoliberalism represents a highly efficient, indeed an intelligent, system for exploiting freedom. Everything that belongs to practices and expressive forms of liberty – emotion, play and communication – comes to be exploited. It is inefficient to exploit people against their will. Allow exploitation yields scant returns. Only when freedom is exploited are returns maximised. [6: 10]

The abuse of freedom highlighted in Han's words is only one aspect belonging to a far more complex sociological and anthropological background characterising the current digital era. Factors such as real or alleged digital narcissists, a language increasingly confined to the medium—the computational machine—a rising technocratic understanding of the human being, all are symptoms that give evidence to an always up-to-date state of crisis. As said before, the current digital society is based on a series of paradoxical conditions, and such aspects lead to a state of crisis continuously in evolution. Once pointed out the existence of chronic crisis characterising the new digital era, it is also interesting highlighting the fact that the word "crisis" originates from the Greek word "krino" which means evaluating, deciding, judging; in other words, a very different meaning compared to the contemporary one. For this reason, with respect to the pertinence of the Greek semantic root and against any possible controversy related to any contemporary meaning, declaring the current digital society in a state of crisis does not mean underlining the perpetuity of the crisis itself, but instead declaring an intent of judgement and proactive decision: in other words, being "within the society, and at the same time against it" [7]. This aspect seems to be the most appropriate attitude to look at the surrounding reality critically, namely being able to look at it from a different point of perspective to reach a more focused understanding of its dynamics.

Connectocracy as socio-political construction in the age of digitisation

The fact that the current digital society lies inside a paradoxical condition requires actions based on evaluation, decision and judgement; in other words, there is the need to elaborate on a new state of crisis. As explained by Thomas Kuhn in his seminal book *The Structure of Scientific Revolutions* [8], the crisis is one of the main symptoms which highlights ongoing translations from ordinary to extraordinary research, the evidence that something highly significant is changing. Applying this theory to the current evolution of our digital society means becoming aware of the fact that being digital is not only a matter of technological development, but first and foremost, it is a matter of human progress. The evolution of the current digital era involves constant changes of horizon, and such changes are affecting both the individual mind and the collective intelligence of the present society, which in return is reducing itself to a sophisticated connective hub.

The translation from a collective society to a new "connective society" is transforming our way to communicate with each other, the way to express our ideas, our perception of public spaces and how we decide to live them. Every passing day, we seem to live in an overabundance of democracy led by everybody and nobody at the same, a new evolutionary system based on a three-dimensional understanding of knowledge possible only in a hyper-connected world, and through the power generated by its connectivity: this is the world of virtual connectivity, a world which can be declared in a condition of *connectocracy*.

The new *connectocratic world* represents the background for the rise of new digital principles. Inside such context, connectivity is sovereign and with it a deformed historical continuity capable of producing new identities. In *connectocracy*, the paradox of decentralization leads to a fragmentary unity made possible only through an unconditional hyper-textuality able to transform knowledge in a multitude of focal points interconnected to each other. Underneath layers of interaction, immersion, and changes, a mutating modulation arises as a new factor for encoding alterations. The stratification of realities finds its natural habitat within the scope of the digital interface, the place where the digital implosion of knowledge—in other words, the hyper-concentration of it due to high levels of connectivity which allow accessing information anywhere, at any time—reaches its maximum point of realisation: *connectocracy* is the power of implosion, the hyper-concentration of everything in every place. If the fact that "we shape our connections and our connections shape us" [9] can be considered an appropriate aphorism for our time, *connectocracy* is the power of connectivity and the influence of such connectivity over any cultural model, anthropological condition, and socio-political construction.

Architecture in *connectocracy*

Several words have been used in describing the current digital society and the rise of *connectocracy* within it. Among them, if we have a closer look at the last paragraph, we can identify eight words particularly suitable for the formulation of operative principles for architecture: connectivity, continuity, decentralisation, immersion, interface, hyper-textuality, modulation, and stratification.

Architecture at the time of *connectocracy* must be an architecture able to incorporate and re-elaborate the rise of new socio-political construction. The eight principles highlighted above might represent a pertinent starting point for an operative architecture in the current digital reality. Such architecture must be an architecture able to synthesising in its design and construction the volatility of an idea, an architecture able to take on the weight of invariants and universal principles. An operative architecture for the digital era will be authentic and progressive if it will be able to realise the primacy of connectivity, the deformation of continuity, the paradox of decentralisation, the measure of immersion, the pragmatism of interface, the hegemony of hyper-textuality, the genetics of modulation, and the interconnection of stratification. Such an intricate design and construction can only be possible inside a built environment characterised by common forms in which common people can recognise themselves.

Eight digital principles for an operative architecture

To better clarify the pertinence of an operative architecture at the time of *connectocracy*, there is a need to provide further explanations about the principles highlighted above. Such explanations collect a series of initial observations on concepts and ideas which will need to be transformed into practical projects to understand better their real value inside a practical construction of an operative architecture.

Connectivity – The translation from a world based on "collective intelligence" [10] into a new one based on "connective intelligence" [11] represents one of the founding principles of the new digital reality. What was initially been able to constitute cultural sedimentations and clear identities able to define a sense of collectivity—initially oral, and then written—is now absorbed into digital networks and proposed through interpretations which do not have any affinity or method of comparison in common with the previous ones. Connectivity is the new human condition that translates collectivity and individuality into the new digital realm making possible the connection in space and time of points otherwise unknown. Transparency, immediacy, plurality are the main features of a new, intelligent surrounding capable of shaping the human mind under the action of connection. The new digital connectivity involves multiplication of mental energies, acceleration of thought, emerging ability to solve problems. It multiplies the degree of social integration and collaboration between individuals throughout the use of hardware and software, which in turn are absorbed to the point of becoming "mindware" of the human mind. Referring to the word "mindware," Derrick de Kerckhove highlights the sociological context in which such new anthropological conditions arise:

Over the past five years, since the invention of virtual reality, the virtualization and convergence of the sensory values, textures, structures, and properties of hardware are turning traditional hardware contents not merely into software but more radically into mindware. [11: 142]

In the world of digital connectivity, connective intelligence represents a dominant factor, and with it, all forms of aggregation and architectural design cannot ignore the influence of connection. To incorporate such influence, architecture must be able to articulate itself through a new configuration of functions connected through a flexible space where different activities are linked in a paratactic and dynamic order. The new degree of connectivity quantifies the architectural space by modelling its nature towards dominant virtuality. Connectivity is the new unit of measurement to codify any architectural surrounding: the higher the degree of connection, the higher the operability of the new digital space.

Continuity – Where "solid electricity" produces light, heat and energy, "liquid electricity" transforms electronic means of production into digital languages of interpretation. The contemporary digital development works in the continuity with the "first machine age" [12], transforming its passive engagement into active disengagement, unyielding commitment into easy escape, discontinuous presence into continuous ubiquity. From a historical perspective, digital continuity is one part of a far more intricate system based on digital totality, a tendency for which the rise of the new digital reality does not intend to eliminate any trace of the past; instead, it focuses its activities on building operative invariants upon which giving life to constant technological development. Digital continuity is based on a primordial totality which is never existed; it is nothing more than an innate relationship between the space of deformation and time of interconnection. Talking about deformation and interconnection, the reference to Deconstructivism is particularly appropriate, and it might represent an inspiring starting point. As explained by Gilles Deleuze and Felix Guattari in their seminal book *Anti-Oedipus: Capitalism and Schizophrenia*:

We no longer believe in an existence made of fragments that, like pieces of an ancient statue, limit their action in waiting for the last piece to arrive so that they can all be pasted together and create an exact unity similar to the original one. We no longer believe in a primordial totality existing in the past, or in a lost totality that is waiting for us in the future. [13: 42]

In such a background of lost totality made of fragments unable to recombine themselves according to the original picture, the traditional concept of continuity—intended as fluid and regular connection in space and time—is no longer enough to describe the current digital present. Digital continuity overturns any traditional meaning of continuity, introjecting the loss of totality and creating a new paradoxical idea of continuity: fragmentary because irreversibly ubiquitous, fluid because continuously interconnected. Architecture may introject such paradoxical continuity by glueing together conceptual fragments from the past inside a new construction technologically oriented to the future.

Decentralisation – In the current state of digital globalisation, there are no more physical or cultural boundaries. Everything is compared and combined, and hybridisation represents the scale of a new identity. Despite an ongoing globalising trend, the magnitude of the historical gap between past and present leads to controversial reactions. Every technological development corresponds to an equal and opposite human evolution; in other words, opposite results to consolidated solutions. In the new digital reality, globalisation is leading to an opposite hyper-localisation, namely a sense of collective protection over the lack of privacy manifested in a hyper-connected world.

We live in a world configured like a "global village"—using Marshall McLuhan's concept—where the situation of being global and local at the same time leads to paradoxical behaviour of human beings: global as the interactive force which characterised the new digital reality, local as the tendency to look into other people's details demanding the protection of our own ones. We live in the wake of an endless "long tail" [14] which leads to a personal fragmentation able to find its way in a background of organised chaos. Following the direction of such a long tail, we find ourselves surrounded by the world around us without looking at it from a defined point of view, but rather through a new desire of immersion and paratactic comparison. We lose authority in favour of engagement, in the name of a tail so long to be understood as a decentralised horizon able to lead to a new "difficult unity." The idea of "difficult unity" is well explained by Robert Venturi in his seminal book *Complexity and Contradiction in Architecture*:

But an architecture of complexity and contradiction has a special obligation toward the whole: its truth must be in its totality or its implications of totality. It must embody the difficult unity of inclusion rather than the easy unity of exclusion. More is not less. [15: 16]

Although digital reality is a reality based on connectivity and decentralisation, the effort to make is to act from a point of inclusion rather than exclusion. Since exclusion is far more complex to reach than inclusion in an endless digital world, the definition of decentralised unity is still possible. Although such unity might seem complicated, paradoxical and fragmentary, it is authentic and realistically digital. Talking about decentralisation in architecture means organising the built environment as an interconnected cluster of polycentric functionalities, recycling any congestion or "junkspace" [16] into sustainable and decentralised urban realities.

Immersion – The electrification of language and the following shift to the current digital immersion leads to the deep penetration of the current digital reality into the human mind. Constant three-dimensional interaction is progressively replacing a static frontality modifying our spatial perception. We feel the need to increase our perceptive senses, and with them, a significant acceleration of thought influences our relationship with the surrounding world. The level of immersion of the new augmented reality not only creates new subjects and configurations, but also it extends the existing ones by accepting the out-of-scale as a generative principle.

The primordial mind-screen immersion is now evolved into a new digital immersion: it is no longer a matter of existing judgments, it is now a matter of creating new ones from scratch. Nowadays, the current digital immersion is configured as an influential factor, and it works together with the digital interface to produce mental penetration of the surrounding environment. As a result, the human mind is considerably extended and able to perceive the existence of parallel digital identities. Day by day, we are experiencing the progressive feeling that the world is no longer over there, distant and detached from us: the digital world is here, under our skin.

To address the rise of immersion in architectural design and production, architecture needs to include new interactive elements, not only as mere technological tools but rather as formal architectural elements able to orient human behaviours. The location of such elements inside the overall architectural composition will dictate how we perceive the space and, with it, the identity and functionality of the space itself.

Interface – The current digital evolution is based on three primary levels of integration: internal (hyper-concentration of received information and acceleration of evaluations), external (intercommunication and networks), interactive (psychological interactivity between the human being and the computational machine in virtual reality). Such technological integration finds in the interface the natural place of exchange, a space not only for acquisition but also evaluation of the digital information received. The interface is the physical place of digital immersion, and interactivity is the central relationship between the human mind and artificial intelligence, bringing to a new psychological connection and virtual partnership between the two. The psychological process of the human mind migrates from a collective perception of the human environment to a case-by-case computerised connection to the digital world.

In such a background characterised by interface and interactivity, the city undertakes a significant transformation. The urban environment stops being the space of human interrelations, a place where social stratifications find their hierarchic order through the production of an architecture based on social codes. Every code has already been revealed in the digital city and, with it, every claim of representation, power or social status. The increasing influence of the digital interface allows the transition from a city-facade—namely a static representation of a consolidated social order—to a city-interface—in other words, a dynamic system dominated by interconnection and the power of networks. Such networks can be considered as links connecting the human mind to the outside world, the medium through which human perception evolves, adapting itself to the surrounding reality. Until the advent of the new digital reality, architecture has been considered a primary discipline for the consolidation of static systems and the representation of motionless social structures. In the age of digitisation, new relationships based on the interface require the configuration of a new adaptable architecture in which the primacy of mobility—intended as spatial flexibility and adaptability—has to guarantee a constant interaction between the human being and the built environment.

Hyper-textuality – Hyper-textuality is the touchstone of the new digital reality, the opportunity to have access to any content anywhere, anytime. Hyper-textuality is the essence of connectivity in the digital world, the ability to continually link remote contents allowing the rise of new three-dimensional knowledge. Things that in the past were orally transmitted—in real-time and through collective sharing—were firstly fragmented and then individualised by written culture and subsequently made multiple, ubiquitous and instantaneous by the advent of the first age of electricity. The contemporary digital evolution extents such instantaneousness of reception through a digital tendency to return multiple and general responses to individual and specific questions.

The digital world is a world based on an implosive and hyper-concentrated knowledge. The definition of "implosive knowledge" refers to the transition from an alphabetic-centred world to a digital-centred one. Before the invention of digital communication—and more in general, before the rise of the first age of electricity—knowledge was concentrated in specific points which most of the time corresponded to libraries or cultural institutions. From one side, such institutions acted as protection for cultural divulgation, while from the other, the use of the alphabet allowed the sedimentation of a culture that was fundamentally oral, namely a culture transmitted in real-time and with a high level of sharing. The advent of writing individualises oral knowledge by expanding it into multiple places of cultural fragmentation. With the advent of electricity—and its current evolution into digitisation—the terms of comparison change and, with them, the advent of a new socio-political and cultural condition. The digital world is dynamic and immersive rather than frontal, static, based on memory such as the alphabetic-centred one. The digital world is based on intelligence no longer collective but rather connective: the digital world is an implosive world.

Hyper-textuality highlights such implosion—it means stratification, interconnection, and integration. It involves new customisation of thinking, turning hardware and software into "mindware". The sedimentation of knowledge no longer originates from periods of incubation, but rather from periods of connection: the amount of what we know is directly proportional to the amount of time that we spend in being connected every day. Zygmunt Bauman well describesthis situation:

If initially the problem was the lack of knowledge, today it is its overabundance. [...] Another collateral damage that is worth highlighting is the loss of ability to think over the long term. [...] Another noteworthy aspect is the loss of the ability to store information in our minds. [...] However, such information, being in a place other than our brain, is not filtered out from our mind; they do not spend a period of incubation or grow in us. In this way, we do not elaborate on them either consciously or unconsciously. [17: 53-6]

Although a new digital perception of knowledge might lead to adverse effects, a new configuration of the human mind comes to attention. With no time for processing new notions and content—either consciously or unconsciously—the mind fails to introject any information, and it continues to project them outwards. The overabundance of inputs in a hyper-textual context makes possible a constant look at knowledge which finds its creative action in the genetic serendipity of its surrounding. A hyper-textual understanding of architecture should be able to consider architecture as spontaneous social construction allowing multiple and unexpected influences, an instrument of expression for a dynamic and malleable knowledge rather than a static and rigid understanding of it. In doing so, the architecture may take several directions, all different but equally valuable in exemplifying the hyper-textuality of the new digital reality.

Modulation – The ubiquity and hyper-connection of the new digital reality are based on digital protocols, codes, semantic nets. The autonomy of the new digital reality is possible through new forms of organisation based on modulation. In a background characterised by modular innovation, digital changes do not only represent signs of technological advancement, but instead, they influence human perception and the remaining part of a mutating collective society. Inside a reality-based on interaction and connectivity, the *connective bit* is the unit of measurement of the digital modulation. The *connective bit* is the basic unit represented by the digital bit plus the influence of such bit over human environment and perception. Through it, any digital modulation is possible, starting from the new digital reality by converting such reality into physical modules. The *connective bit* has an unstable nature, self-organising, ubiquitous. Its genetics is based on plasticity and malleability, allowing active contact with the surrounding reality, a condition able to absorb the surrounding context. Due to the mutating nature of the *connective bit*, the idea itself of digital module moves from the codification of a generative element to the consideration of a generated one, namely a component in evolution where the beginning never matches the end. In doing so, the module itself does no longer represent a generating unit but rather the result of a genetic mutation.

For this reason, inside a new architectural perspective in the current digital reality, creating a new modular system can no longer represent a linear process. A new "digital Modulor" can only be possible if intended as a mutant and immersive modular system able to accept genetic alteration as identity and generative principle. Digital modulation is a mutating system constantly in progress.

Stratification– Digital reality is a stratified reality. It derives from a sedimentary stratification of collective culture, and currently, its identity is translated into a malleable stratification, continually moving and evolving inside the digital world. The layers of the new digital space are layers of interaction, immersion and mutation. They originate from the technological nature of any new virtual construction, adapting themselves into the physical realm to which they refer. The digital stratification subordinates its nature to a configuration no longer formed by well-defined layers but rather a mix of levels organised as spatial interstices without a pre-set hierarchy. The layers of the new digital world are formed by generative datasets modified according to their adaptability and interaction with the surrounding reality. Digital stratification is not just a matter of data and information, but instead, it is rooted in the connective nature of the new virtual reality. Architecture may introject stratification inside its conception by working on malleable levels, their repetition and interaction with each other, and the way they relate to the surrounding context. As a distinctive feature in contemporary digital reality, stratification might represent an appropriate principle to order and organise a paratactic interaction between architectural elements.

Conclusion: towards an operative architecture

The eight digital principles explained so far represent one of the possible starting point for the formulation of an operative architecture. Such explanations are only initial observations limited to the length of a single paper. The complexity and semantic plurality of such principles require a far more comprehensive analysis able to conduct further research for the translation of such principles into a practical methodology of architectural conception.

For now, it is important to highlight the existence of a possible architectural paradigm, and it is essential to consider architecture—even the most digital and computationally evolved one—as a matter of human progress rather than mere technological development. Such an approach allows finding ideas that can be converted into operative principles, and the existence of operative principles represents an essential condition in the current digital reality, since the lack of ideas and operative concepts leads to a continuous specialisation and clusterisation of knowledge, and with them to the loss of any ability to look at things holistically.

In the age of *connectocracy*, architecture is the sedimentation of technological development inside a background of human progress. Concerning the new digital reality, the current state of architecture is still a matter of avant-garde, a symptom of transaction towards an identity still to come. Concentrating the complexity of an era into principles may easily lead to an excessive level of reduction, but a certain level of reduction represents a necessary action to bring the attention of advanced architectural research back to humanities; in other words, taking the advancement of research back to basics, back to human needs.

The analysis conducted through the paper has highlighted the rise of a possible architecture inside the new *connectocratic society*, and the existence of eight principles in such society represent initial signs of a potentially rich background for further research in architectural design and construction, in a time where digital futures are arising.

[1] Benedikt, M., *Cyberspace: First Steps*, The MIT Press, 1991.

[2] Lévy, P., *Cyberculture. Rapport au Conseil de l'Europe*, Edition Odile Jacob, 1997.

[3] McLuhan, M. and Fiore, Q., *The Medium is the Message. An Inventory of Effects*, Bantam Books, 1967.

[4] Greenfield, A., *Radical Technologies: The Design of Everyday Life*, Verso Books, 2017, 89.

[5] Han, B., *The Transparency Society*, Stanford University Press, 2015.

[6] Han, B., *Psychopolitics: Neoliberalism and New Technologies of Power*, Verso Books, 2017.

[7] Tronti, M., *Operai e Capitale*, Einaudi, 1966, 4.

[8] Kuhn, T., *The Structure of Scientific Evolution*, University of Chicago Press, 1962.

[9] Mitchell, W., *The City of Bits: Space, Place and the Infobahn*, The MIT Press, 1995, 49.

[10] Lévy, P., *Collective Intelligence. Mankind's Emerging World in Cyberspace*, Perseus Books, 1997.

[11] De Kerckhove, D., *Connected Intelligence. The Arrival of the Web Society*, Somerville House Publishing, 1997.

[12] Banham, R., *Theory and Design in the First Machine Age, The Architectural Press*, 1960.

[13] Deleuze, G. and Guattari, F., *Capitalisme et Schizophrénie. Anti-Oedipe*, Les Editions de Minuit, 1972.

[14] Anderson, C., *The Long Tail: Why the Future of Business Is Selling Less of More*, Hyperion, 2006.

[15] Venturi, R., *Complexity and Contradiction in Architecture*, The Museum of Modern Art, New York, 1966.

[16] Koolhaas, R., *Junkspace*, Quodlibet, 2006.

[17] Bauman, Z., *La Vita tra Reale e Virtuale*, Mattei, M. (Ed.), Egea, 2014.

projects

PRIMITIVE VOXELS

From deconstruction to non-pedigreed spaces

Combining algorithmic processes based on particle growth systems and mesh optimisation procedures, the research project intends to investigate into the formation of deconstructive spaces converting their nature of "signature spaces" into autonomous mesh configurations generated by computational processes, and therefore oriented toward the formation of anonymous assemblies and non-pedigreed spaces. The use of the word "pedigreed" related to architecture refers to research conducted in the field of primitive settlements and constructions, a time where architects did not exist, and the built environment was shaped by the work of anonymous builders. Nowadays, computers can be considered as the most prominent of such anonymous builders in the current digital era, and computational procedures lead towards similar although asymmetrical anonymous results.

The project is based on an algorithmic process divided into two main phases: design and optimisation. In terms of design, the creation of a first algorithm based on particles growth allows to covert the edges of 3D elements into particles that automatically duplicate themselves following specific rules based on movement and reciprocal distance. The obtained particles are then converted into voxels to complete the volumetric fragmentation of the original space. Such a process leads to the result of generating a voxelated space where the original hierarchy between elements is transformed into a paratactic assembly of voxels. Once the design phase is completed, the voxels are blended into a single mesh which is then optimised through an algorithm based on tessellation solutions obtained through the use of a custom C# library. Finally, after the optimisation procedures, the mesh is analysed to control the area and the number of faces that can be potentially converted into panels and self-bearing structures for construction purposes.

The research project has allowed experimenting with an algorithmic process that has been able to provide a different point of view through which reconsidering deconstruction in architecture. The deconstructive space has been intended as one of the last expressions of authentic human-centric creativity in architecture—the creativity of the "archistar"—which is

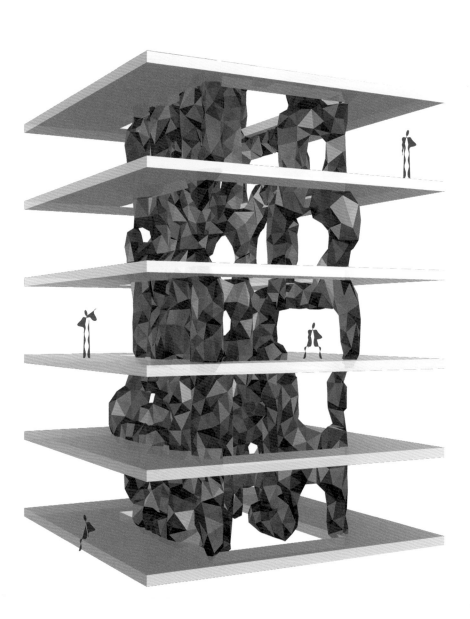

NON-PEDIGREED ARCHITECTURE

now progressively replaced by autonomous and self-generative computational processes. The result leads to the generation of continuous and immersive spaces, and it reflects an ongoing process inside the architectural discipline where architects stop being the final creator of design solutions to become mere initiators of computational processes, leading towards autonomous and unexpected results. For this reason, the research project intends to highlight the shift from a "pedigreed architecture"—or architecture of the "archistar", such as deconstructive architecture—to a "non-pedigreed architecture"—or architecture without architects.

PSEUDOCODE

[PART 1] PARTICLE SYSTEM

#.1 Input curve and instantiate list of particles
```
set curve
get points along the curve = list point particles
```

#.2 Instantiate list of vectors for particle movement
```
set list vector movements
for (i -> particles)
    add vector 0 to movements
```

#.3 Set rule for movement
```
for (i -> particles)
    for (j = i + 1 -> particles)
        get double distance between i and j
        if (distance > set double maxDistance)
            continue
        get vector movement = distance
        set double speed
        get vector movementIncrement = (max distance -
            distance) * set speed
        add movementIncrement to movements
```

#.4 Add average movement to particles
```
for (i -> particles)
    get vector averageMove = movements / particles
```

```
        i += averageMove
```

#.5 Create new particles
```
    set list int splitIndices
    set list point newParticles


    for (i -> particles - 1)
        if (distance > maxDstance)
            get int splitIndex (i + 1)
            add splitIndex to splitIndeces


    foreach (index in splitIndices)
        get point newParticle
        add newParticle to newParticles
```

#.6 Create voxels
```
    set list mesh voxels
    for (i -> particles)
        get mesh voxel
        add voxel to voxels
```

#.7 Set rule for voxel addition and removal
```
    set double voxelX
    set double voxelY
    set double voxelZ
    get voxelSize = voxelX * voxelY * voxelZ
    get distance between voxel [i] and
        voxel [i + 1]
    if (distance < voxelSize)
        remove voxel[i] from voxels
    else if (distance = voxelSize)
        add voxel[i] to voxels
    else
        continue
```

#.8 Results
```
    get newParticles
    get voxels
```


[PART 2] MESH OPTIMISATION

* The optimisation has been conducted through the open source C#
library geometry3Sharp.

#.1 Covert input mesh to G3 mesh
get G3 mesh from input mesh

#.2 Compute first optimisation procedure
set G3 mesh autoRepair function
set G3 mesh holeFill function
set G3 mesh constraints to geometry target

#.3 Compute second optimisation procedure
set G3 mesh removeFinTriangle function
set G3 mesh removeIsolateTriangle function
set G3 mesh removeUnusedVertices function
set G3 mesh removeAllBowtieVertices function

#.4 Apply G3 reducer to optimised mesh
set G3 mesh reducer
if (reducer)
   set G3 mesh reducer triangle count
   set G3 mesh reducer triangle edge length
     set min triangle edge length
     set max triangle edge length

   set G3 mesh reducer preserveBoundaryShape
    function
   set G3 mesh reducer SetProjectionTarget function

   return reduced mesh

#.5 Apply G3 remesher to reduced mesh
set G3 mesh remesher
if (remesher)
   set G3 mesh remesher precompute function
   set G3 mesh remesher setProjectionTarget
    function
   set G3 projection mode to Inline

   set G3 mesh remesher enableFlip function
   set G3 mesh remesher preventNormalFlips
    function
   set G3 mesh remesher setTargetEdgeLength
    function

#.6 Enable mesh smoothing
   set G3 mesh remesher enableSmoothing function
   set G3 mesh remesher SmoothSpeedT funtion

```
for (i -> remesherIteration)
    set G3 mesh remesher BasicRemeshPass
        function
    set min triangle edge length
    set max triangle edge length


return remeshed mesh
```

#.7 Convert from G3 mesh to Rhino mesh
```
get Rhino mesh from G3 reduced mesh
get Rhino mesh from G3 remeshed mesh
```

#.8 Results
```
get Rhino reduced mesh;
get Rhino remeshed mesh;
```

[PART 3] MESH ANALYSIS

#.1 Create lists to store input values
```
set list double panelsArea
set list int panelsCount
```

#.2 Add values to lists
```
foreach (area in panelsArea)
    for (i -> panelsArea)
        get panelsArea [i];
        get panelsCount + 1;
```

#.3 Set min and max values
```
set minValue
set maxValue
```

#.4 Check area values against min and max values
```
for(i -> panelsArea)
    get minArea = Min(minValue, i)
    get maxArea = Max(maxValue, i)
```

#.5 Results
```
get panelsArea
get panelsCount
get minArea
get maxArea
```

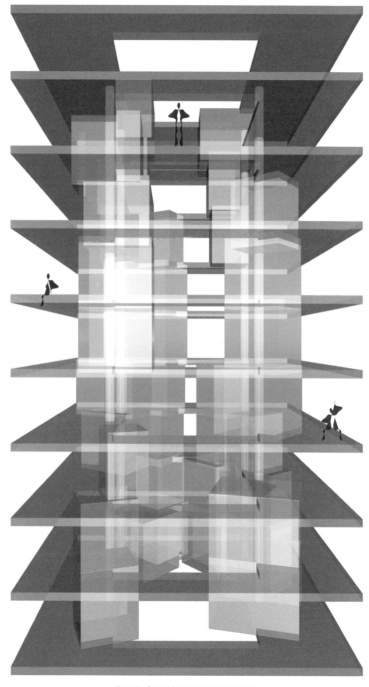

[STEP 1] DECONSTRUCTIVE SPACE

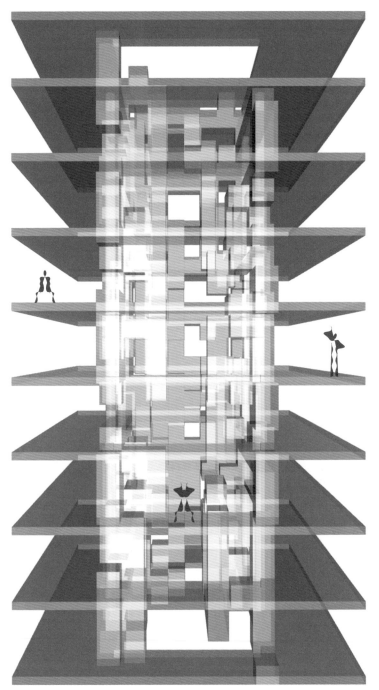

[STEP 2] VOXELISATION

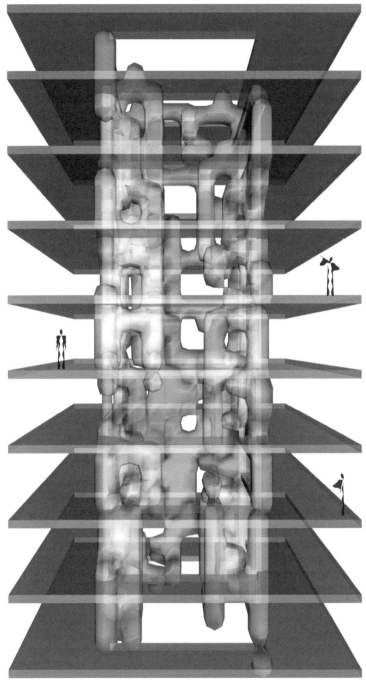

[STEP 3] BLENDING VOXELS

[STEP 4] NON-PEDIGREED SPACE

MAISON DE CUBES

From hierarchical elements to equal components

The project *Maison de Cubes* combines topology optimisation and voxelisation inside the design of a flexible and repeatable building structure. The research intends to investigate the formation of architectural constructions where the hierarchy between structural elements is substituted by a modular system formed by equal components. The title of the project refers to Le Corbusier's Maison Dom-Ino, which has been used as the starting point for the computational process. This choice reflects the intention to apply the research on consolidated construction systems to highlight the different level of architectural language produced by algorithmic procedures. In doing so, the original principles guiding the Maison Dom-Ino are conceptually stretched and translated into their new digital format: in other words, from mass production of houses able to combine themselves into series like dominoes—such as in Le Corbusier's idea—to mass production of components able to combine themselves into houses like Lego blocks.

The project is based on an algorithmic procedure referring to two main processes: topology optimisation and voxelisation. After having recreated the Maison Dom-Ino in a 3D environment, all the elements of the original Le Corbusier's project are optimised through the use of an algorithm that allows achieving the same structural performance by using around half the amount of concrete through the use of targeted topology optimisation. The output of such topology optimisation is a plastic mesh where all the architectural elements are affected by computational forces able to erode the original shape. Once all the elements have been optimised, the complexity of the generated mesh is converted into cubes—voxels—through the use of voxelisation algorithms. The final result is a house in which all the elements are converted into cubes giving life to a modular system easy to combine through technologies available for automated assembly. The generated architecture is an architecture without hierarchy, an architecture where elements are blended according to linguistic mixology, referring to the hypertextual language of the current digital era.

The research project has allowed experimenting with an algorithmic procedure that has been able to provide a different point of view through

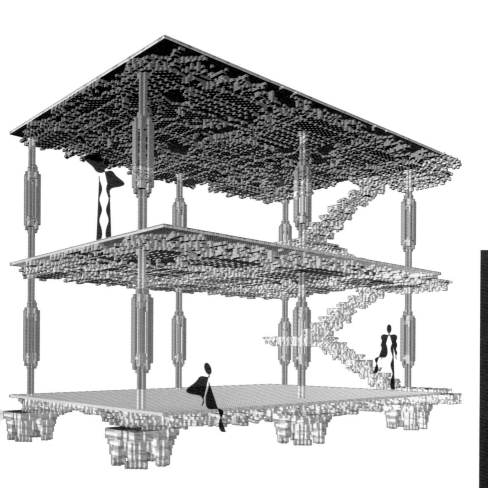

FROM MAISON DOM-INO TO MAISON DE CUBES

which considering architectural elements in the current digital era. In a time where everything seems melted inside the levelling nature of digital reality, architecture has to reconsider the traditional conception of its fundamental elements to be able to develop them into a more equalitarian composition. In doing so, an entirely new architectural language may arise as the touchstone of an ongoing shift affecting architectural design and construction.

PSEUDOCODE

[PART 1] TOPOLOGY OPTIMISATION

```
#.1 Set geometry as initial domain
    set mesh geometry
    set double density
    set double materialProperties

    get list mesh inputGeometry
    get double boundaryDomain

    for (i -> inputGeometry)
        if (density - 1 < i)
            add density to boundaryDomain

#.2 Set volume load
    set mesh loadVolume
    set vector loadDirection
    set list mesh loadVolumes

    if (loadVolume is not closed)
        return error
    else
        add loadVolume to loadVolumes

#.3 Set support geometry
    get list mesh loadVolumes
```

```
set list mesh supportGeometries
set bool applySupport

for (i -> supportGeometries)
    if (!supportGeometries = null)
        applySupport = true
        get union supportGeometries

foreach geometry in supportGeometries
    set list point supportedPoints
    set point supportedPt
    add supportedPt to supportedPoints
```

#.4 Create topological model
```
get data boundaryDomain
get data supportGeometries
set double modelResolution
set data topologicalModel

if (boundaryDomain || supportGeometries = null)
    return error
else
    get topologicalModel
```

#.5 Connect topological model to engine solver

* For the optimisation process has been used the engine solver *Optimus* from the GH plug-in *Topos* which is based on Bendsoe and Sigmund's theorem using optimality criteria algorithm to update density

```
get topologicalModel
set data analyserParameters
set data optimusParameters

get optimisedModel from engine solver
```

#.6 Repeat optimisation procedure for all elements
```
set list mesh optimisedGeometries
add optimisedGeometry to optimisedGeometries
```

#.7 Results
```
get list mesh optimisedGeometries
```

[PART 2] VOXELISATION

#.1 Get mesh from topology optimisation
```
get data list mesh optimisedGeometries
```

#.2 Create voxels grid
```
set box boundingBox
set point voxelPt
set voxelSize (xVoxel, yVoxel, zVoxel)
set array voxelGrid
set array optimisedGeometriesGrid

For (i -> optimisedGeometriesGrid)
    optimisedGeometriesGrid[i] = voxelGrid

set boundingBox and voxelPt
get voxelsGrid (voxelGrid * voxelSize)
optimisedGeometriesGrid = voxelsGrid
```

#.3 Apply voxels grid to mesh
```
set data list mesh optimisedGeometries
set list box voxels
set voxelsGrid

if (voxelsGrid = null)
    return error
else
    foreach geometry in optimisedGeometries
        cast geometry to box
        add box to voxels
```

#.4 Results
```
get voxels
```

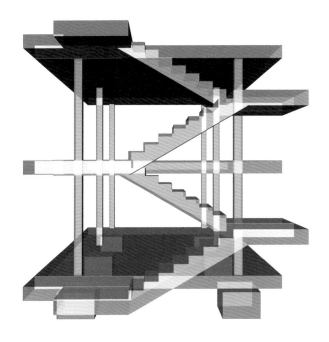

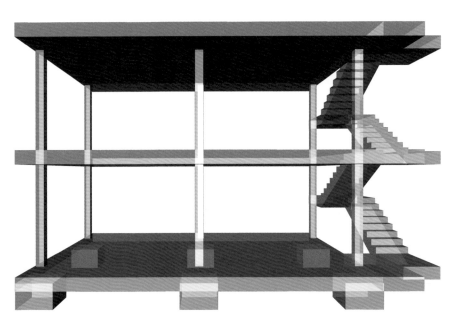

[STEP 1] MAISON DOM-INO

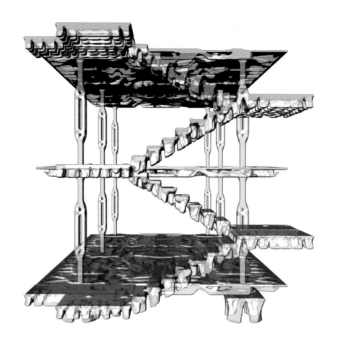

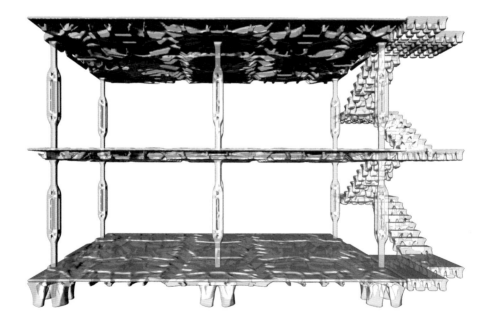

[STEP2] TOPOLOGY OPTIMISATION

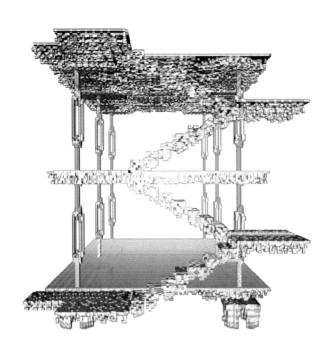

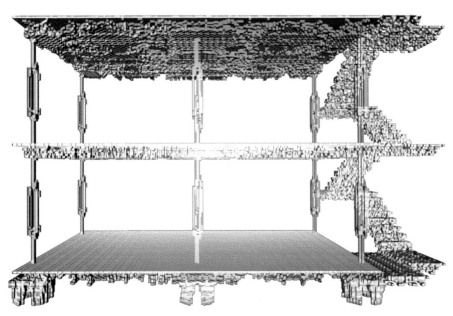

[STEP 3] VOXELISATION

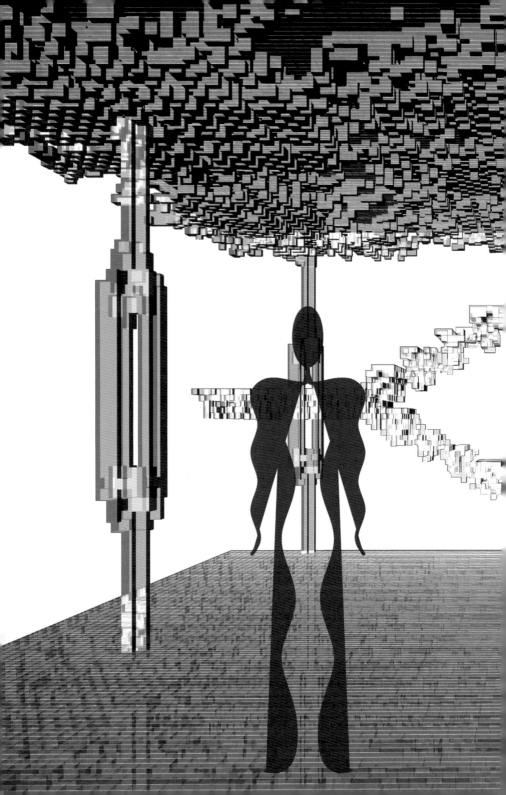

MUNDANEUM OF THE DIGITAL KNOWLEDGE

From distinctive functions to typological mixology

The project *Mundaneum of the Digital Knowledge* combines cellular automaton models and voxelisation procedures inside the design and conception of a public building. The research intends to work on the idea of public buildings as a conglomeration of clusterised digital knowledge. The starting point is the idea of Mundaneum—initially called *Palais Mondial* ("world palace")—developed by the Belgian lawyers Paul Otlet and Henri La Fontaine at the turn of the 20th century. The Mundaneum was an institution having the purpose of collecting all the world's knowledge under the same roof; in other words, a sort of large container of knowledge where everything was gathered and linked. In this case, the project intends to re-elaborate the holistic idea underlining the original project into a new architectural composition.

The project is based on an algorithmic procedure referring to two main processes: cellular automaton models and voxelisation algorithms. After having set the rules for the cellular automaton model, the perimeter of the building is decided and used as the starting point for the initiation of the cellular automaton growth. Once the generic volumetric structure is created, voxelisation algorithms divide the structure into voxels set to a specific size, and then such voxels are progressively replaced by standardised architectural components. The algorithmic procedure allows for the creation of a building where all the parts are connected according to a stratified order following the functionality of the different clusters of knowledge that constitute the *Mundaneum*. In doing so, spaces and functions are blended according to the uses promoted by the new digital society, a sort of typological mixology under construction for the formation of a possible architectural machine.

The research project has allowed experimenting with an algorithmic procedure that has been able to test a different architectural composition based on standardised and clusterised systems. Such systems may be easily suitable for automation and robotic assembly, giving life to a data-based architecture where specific sets of data replace traditional architectural models. The project highlights the fact that a new architectural language is possible to identify the current digital era. Such language

MUNDANEUM OF THE DIGITAL KNOWLEDGE

may be based on paratactic assemblies and typological mixology for the formation of an architecture able to reflect the panoptic hybridisation and socio-cultural levelling promoted by the real nature of being digital.

PSEUDOCODE

[PART 1] CELLULAR AUTOMATA

```
#.1 Declare variables
    set list point caPts
    set list box caBoxes
    set int xStart
    set int yStart
    set int zLayers


#.2 Set booleans for CA currentState and nextState
    set bool currentState
    set bool nextState


#.3 Create glider and starting conditions
    set double initX
    set double initY
    set void (currentState, initX, initY)
        currentState 1 = true
        currentState 2 = false
        currentState 3 = true
        ...
    for (i -> xStart)
        currentState = new bool (yStart)
        nextState = new bool (yStart)
        for (j -> yStart)
            currentState = false


#.4 Set boxes for live cells
    for (i -> xStart)
        for (j -> yStart)
```

```
if (currentState)
    set double xBoxSize
    set double yBoxSize
    set double zBoxSize
    get point caPt
    add caPt to caPts
    get plane pBox from caPt
    get interval iBox
    get box caBox (pBox, iBox, iBox, iBox)
    add caBox to caBoxes
```

#.5 Count alive neightbours
```
set int caActive
for (i -> -/+ 1)
    for (j -> -/+ 1)
        if (i != null && j != null)
            get currentState = true
            caActive++
```

#.6 Set next generation conditions
```
if (caActive = [set conditions])
    nextState = true
else if (caActive = [set conditions])
    nextState = false
else
    nextState = currentState
```

#.7 Replace currentState with nextState
```
for (i -> xStart)
    for (j -> yStart)
        currentState = nextState
```

#.8 Results
```
get caBoxes;
```

[PART 2] VOXELISATION

#.1 Set list mesh from caBoxes
```
set list mesh caBoxes
get list point caBoxesCenters
```

#.2 Import 3d model of base component
```
set mesh baseModule
```

```
#.3 Get face center points and assembly direction lines
    foreach face in baseModule
        get point faceCenter
        get list line faceEdges
        for (i -> faceEdges)
            set line directionLine (faceCenter, faceEdges[i])


#.4 Set list mesh for final voxel components
    set list mesh finalVoxels


#.5 Replace CA voxels with base components
    foreach caBox in caBoxes
        set point caBoxesCenter
        set point baseModuleCenter
        if (caBoxesCenter = baseModuleCenter)
        caBoxes = baseModule
        add baseModule to finalVoxels


#.6 Set rotation rule
    set list point baseModuleCenters
    set double angle
    set Random rndRotation
    for (i -> finalVoxels)
        get baseModuleCenters[i]
        rotate finalVoxels[i] = (angle * rndRotation,
        baseModuleCenters[i])


#.7 Results
    get finalVoxels
```

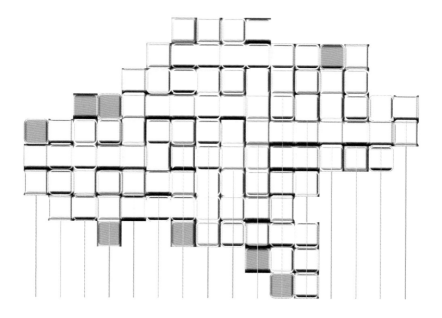

MUNDANEUM OF THE DIGITAL KNOWLEDGE: PLAN & ELEVATION

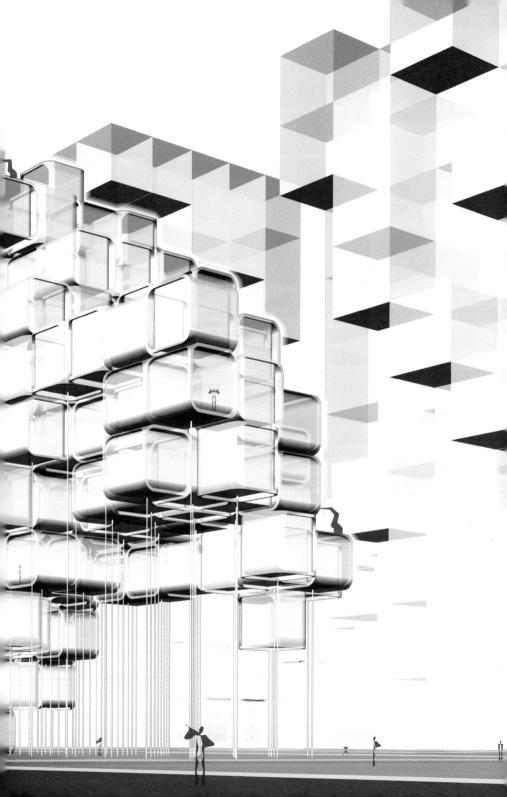

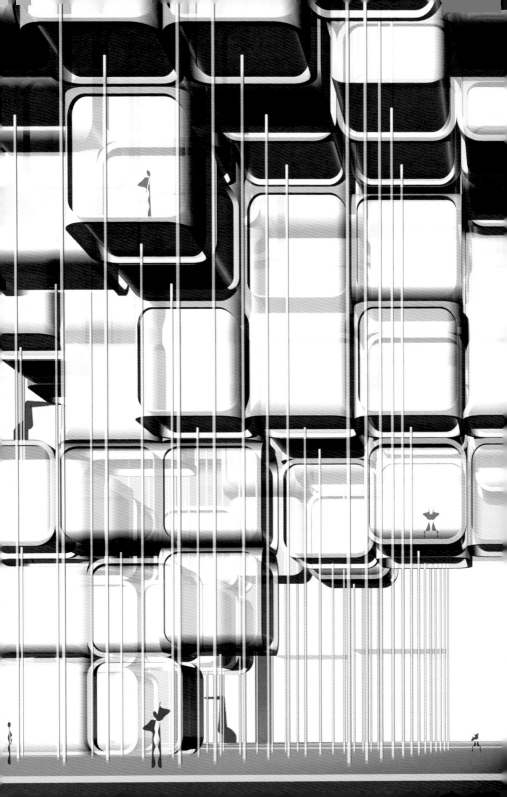

THE PARATACTIC CITY

From socio-cultural urbanity to urban parataxis

The Paratactic City combines L-system algorithms with voxelisation procedures inside the design of a paratactic urban environment. The research intends to investigate the formation of urban settlements where the traditional idea of the city as a combination of distinct and well-defined social, cultural and political structures is overturned by the generative and disruptive force of computational processes and automated fabrication. The choice of using simple and recursive voxelised components reflects the intention to apply the research on recognisable construction systems highlighting the appropriateness of the combination of procedural cities and robotic assemblies. In doing so, the urban environment generated by the computational procedure is an anonymous land where the action of robots can easily fit into the construction of a new paratactic urban identity.

The project is based on an algorithmic procedure referring to two main processes: L-systems and voxelisation. After having decided the computational rules dictating the L-system adopted for the generation of both streets and buildings, the algorithm runs through a series of pre-defined iterations and the procedural city is generated in all its parts. Once the main parts are set, urban spaces are obtained from the empty areas formed by the L-system algorithm, while building volumes are randomised and populated with points that are used to place voxels. The result is a series of recursive structures dictating a final urban configuration that can easily accommodate robotic assembly and automation procedures for the construction of both private and public urban spaces and buildings.

The research project has allowed experimenting with an algorithmic procedure that has been able to provide a different perspective for urban design in the age of digitisation. The paratactic tendency of being digital may be incorporated inside the construction of a new idea of the city where every hierarchical order between buildings, streets, and urban spaces is mixed together according to a new urban identity based on equalisation, continuity and connectivity promoted by the rise of the digital interface. *The Paratactic City* is the city of architecture without architects, a place for the rise of a new non-geometrical, data-based architecture, where specific sets of data replace traditional architectural models. For this reason,

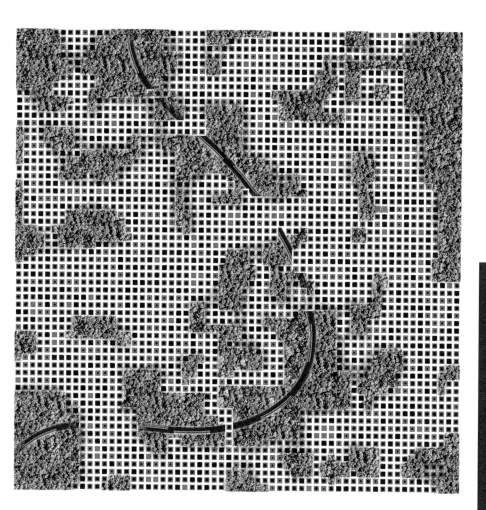

THE PARATACTIC CITY: PLAN

The Paratactic City represents a work-in-progress idea of architectural pa-rataxis reflecting the anthropological levelling promoted by the current digital society, a phenomenon achievable and understandable through the use of computation and automated fabrication, and the belief that ro-bots might become the new anonymous builders of the future basing their independence on the novelty promoted by the new genetic complexity of computational processes.

PSEUDOCODE

[PART 1] L-SYSTEM

```
#.1 Set L-System axiom
    set string axiom

#.2 Set L-System rules
    set dictionary L-SystemRules <char, string rule>

#.3 Set project variables
    set list outputPoints
    set double distanceBetweenPts
    set point startingPoint
    set vector startingVector
    set double rotationAngle

    set string L-SystemSentence
    set int numberOfIterations
    set bool iteration

#.4 Set L-System drawing rules
    set list L-SystemPoints
    set list L-SystemMovingVector

    for (i -> L-SystemSentence)
        get char in L-SystemSentence
        if(char1)
```

```
    set drawing rule 1
if(char2)
    set drawing rule 2
if(char3)
    set drawing rule 3
...
if(lastChar)
    set last drawing rule
```

#.5 Set L-Sytem updating rules
```
set string nextL-SystemSentence
for (i -> L-SystemSentence)
    get char in L-SystemSentence
    set bool charFound

    for (i -> L-SystemRules)
        if (charFound)
            update nextL-SystemSentence
        if (!charFound)
            nextL-SystemSentence += char

    update L-SystemSentence with nextL-SystemSentence
    call L-System drawing rules function
```

#.6 Set L-System starting conditions
```
set numberOfIteration = 0
set axiom
set startingVector
set startingPoint
set distanceBetweenPts

clear list outputPoints
call L-System drawing rules function
```

#.7 Set L-System updating conditions
```
if (iteration)
    update numberOfIterations
    clear outputPoints
    call L-System updating rules function
```

#.8 Results
```
get outputPoints;
```

[PART 2] VOXELISATION

#.1 Create data set from outputPoints
    get data list outputPoints

#.2 Set range of values for building volumes
    set Interval xSize
    set Interval ySize
    set Interval zSize

#.3 Randomize building volumes and populate them with points
    set list buildings
    set Random buildingsRnd

    foreach point in outputPoints
        buildingsRnd (xSize, ySize, zSize)
        get box building
        add building to list buildings

    for (i -> buildings)
        set list populationPts
        set Random populationPtsRnd
        get volume building[i]
        get point in volume building[i]
        add point to populationPts

#.4 Create list of voxels and set voxel size and index
    set list mesh voxels
    set double voxelSize
    set int voxelIndex

#.5 Apply voxel to each point
    foreach point in populationPts
        set double voxelX = get point.X * (1.0 / voxelSize);
        set double voxelY = get point.Y * (1.0 / voxelSize);
        set double voxelZ = get point.Z * (1.0 / voxelSize);
        get mesh voxel (voxelSize, voxelX, voxelY, voxelZ);
        add voxel to list voxels

#.7 Results
    get mesh voxels

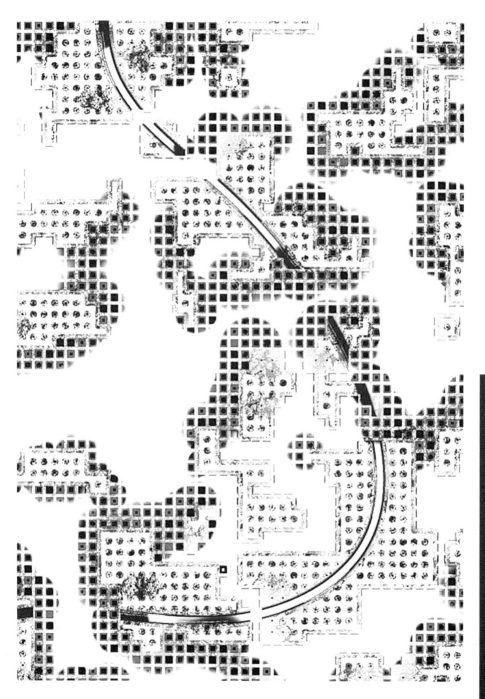

THE PARATACTIC CITY: SERENDIPIC MAP

appendix

Bibliography

The publications listed below have been consulted during the preparatory studies of the papers. The following list has to be intended as an additional compendium to the specific references mentioned at the end of each paper.

[1]   Andrew Adamatzky and Genaro J. Martinez (Eds.), *Designing Beauty: The Art of Cellular Automata*, Springer 2016.

[2]   Christopher Alexander, *Notes on the Synthesis of Form*, Harvard University Press, Cambridge MA and London 1964.

[3]   Chris Anderson, *The Long Tail: Why the Future of Business Is Selling Less of More*, Hyperion, New York 2006.

[4]   Paola Antonelli, *Mutant Materials in Contemporary Design*, The Museum of Modern Art, New York 1995.

[5]   William Ross Ashby, *An Introduction to Cybernetics*, Chapman & Hall, London 1957.

[6]   Drew Ayers, *Spectacular Posthumanism. The Digital Vernacular of Visual Effects*, Bloomsbury Academic, New York and London 2019.

[7]   Stephen Barr, *Experiments in Topology*, John Murray, London 1965.

[8]   Zygmunt Bauman, *Liquid Modernity*, Polity Press and Blackwell Publishers, Cambridge and Oxford 2000.

[9]   Zygmunt Bauman, *La Vita tra Reale e Virtuale*, Maria Grazia Mattei (Ed.), Egea, Milano 2014.

[10] Martin P. Bendsøe and Ole Sigmund, *Topology Optimization. Theory, Methods and Applications*, Springer, Berlin and New York 2003.

[11] Michael Benedikt, *Cyberspace: First Steps*, The MIT Press, Cambridge MA and London 1991.

[12] Peter J. Bentley (Ed.), *Evolutionary Design by Computers*, Morgan Kaufmann Publishers, San Francisco 1999.

[13] Peter J. Bentley and David W. Corne (Eds.), *Creative Evolutionary Systems*, Academic Press, London and San Diego 2002.

[14] Henriette Bier (Ed.), *Robotic Building*, Springer 2018.

[15] Marco Biraghi and Alberto Ferlenga (Eds.), *Architettura del Novecento. Teorie, Scuole, Eventi*, Einaudi, Torino 2012.

[16] Marco Biraghi, *L'Architetto come Intellettuale*, Einaudi, Torino 2019.

[17] Marco Biraghi and Giovanni Damiani, *Le Parole dell'Architettura. Un'Antologia di Testi Teorici e Critici: 1945-2000*, Einaudi, Torino 2009.

[18] Trevor J. Blank (Ed.), *Folklore and the Internet. Vernacular Expression in a Digital World*, Utah State University Press, Logan 2009.

[19] Margaret Boden, *The Creative Mind. Myths and Mechanisms*, Weidenfeld and Nicolson, London 1990.

[20] Sigrid Brell-Cokcan and Johannes Braumann (Eds.), *Robotic Fabrication in Architecture, Art and Design 2012*, Springer, Wien and New York 2012.

[21] Tommaso Brighenti, *Pedagogie Architettoniche. Scuole, Didattica, Progetto*, Accademia University Press, Torino 2018.

[22] Lucy Bullivant (Ed.), *4dspace: Interactive Architecture*, AD «Architectural Design», January-February 2005, Profile 173.

[23] Mark Burry, *Scripting Cultures. Architectural Design and Programming*, AD Primers, Wiley, London 2011.

[24] Jane Burry, Jenny Sabin, Bob Sheil and Marilena Skavara (Eds.), *Fabricate 2020*, UCL Press, London 2020.

[25] Lucas Capelli and Vicente Guallart, *Self Sufficient City: Envisioning the Habitat of the Future*, Actar, Barcelona 2010.

[26] Mario Carpo and Frédérique Lemerle (Eds.), *Perspective, Projections & Design. Technologies of Architectural Representation*, Routledge, London and New York 2008.

[27] Mario Carpo, *The Alphabet and the Algorithm*, The MIT Press, Cambridge MA and London 2011.

[28] Mario Carpo (Ed.), *The Digital Turn in Architecture 1992-2012*, AD Reader, Wiley, London 2013.

[29] Mario Carpo, *The Second Digital Turn. Design Beyond Intelligence*, The MIT Press, Cambridge MA and London 2017.

[30] Noam Chomsky, *Syntactic Structure*, Walter de Gruyter, Berlin 1957.

[31] Molly Claypool, Manuel Jimenez Garcia, Gilles Retsin and Vicente Soler, *Robotic Building. Architecture in the Age of Automation*, Edition Detail, Munich 2019.

[32] Paul Coates, *Programming. Architecture*, Routledge, London and New York 2010.

[33] Peter Cook, *Architecture Workbook: Designing Through Motive*, Wiley, London 2016.

[34] Nigel Cross, *The Automated Architect*, Piom, London 1977.

[35] Renato De Fusco, *Architettura come Mass Medium. Note per una Semiologia Architettonica*, Dedalo, Bari 1967.

[36] Derrick De Kerckhove, *The Skin of Culture. Investigating the New Electronic Reality*, Somerville House Publishing, Toronto 1995.

[37] Derrick De Kerckhove, *Connected Intelligence. The Arrival of the Web Society*, Somerville House Publishing, Toronto 1997.

[38] Derrick De Kerckhove, *Psicotecnologie Connettive*, Maria Grazia Mattei (Ed.), Egea, Milano 2014.

[39] Derrick De Kerckhove and Cristina Miranda De Almeida (Eds.), *The Point of Being*, Cambridge Scholars Publishing, Newcastle upon Tyne 2014

[40] Gilles Deleuze and Felix Guattari, *Capitalisme et Schizophrénie. L'Anti-Oedipe*, Les Editions de Minuit, Paris 1972.

[41] Christian Derix and Asmund Izaki (Eds.), *Empathic Space. The Computation of Human-Centric Architecture*, AD «Architectural Design», September-October 2014, Profile 231.

[42] Hubert L. Dreyfus and Stuart E. Dreyfus with Tom Athanasiou, *Mind Over Machine. The Power of Human Intuition and Expertise in the Era of the Computer*, The Free Press, New York 1986.

[43] Nick Dunn, *Digital Fabrication in Architecture*, Laurence King Publishing, London 2012.

[44] Peter Eisenman, *Diagram Diaries*, Thames & Hudson, London 1999.

[45] Jacques Ellul, *The Technological Society*, Vintage Books, New York 1964.

[46] Andrew Feenberg, *Questioning Technology*, Routledge, London 1999.

[47] Paul Feyerabend, *Against Method. Outline of an Anarchistic Theory of Knowledge*, Verso, London 1975.

[48] Gary William Flake, *The Computational Beauty of Nature. Computer Explorations of Fractals, Chaos, Complex Systems, and Adaptation*, The MIT Press, Cambridge MA and London 1998.

[49] Wendy W Fok and Antoine Picon (Eds.), *Digital Property. Open-Source Architecture*, AD «Architectural Design», September-October 2016, Profile 243.

[50] John Frazer, *An Evolutionary Architecture*, Architectural Association Press, London 1995.

[51] Thomas Friedman, *The World is Flat. A Brief History of the Globalized World in the 21st Century*, Penguin Books, New York and London 2005.

[52] Luca Galofaro, *Digital Eisenman. An Office of the Electronic Age*, Birkhäuser, Basel 1999.

[53] Neil Gershenfeld, *When Things Start to Think*, Coronet Books, London 1999.

[54] James Gleick, *Chaos. Making a New Science*, Cardinal, London 1988.

[55] Ruairi Glynn and Bob Sheil (Eds.), *Fabricate 2011*, UCL Press, London 2011.

[56] Fabio Gramazio and Matthias Kohler (Eds.), *Made by Robots: Challenging Architecture at a Larger Scale*, AD «Architectural Design», May-June 2014, Profile 229.

[57] Fabio Gramazio, Matthias Kohler and Silke Langenberg (Eds.), *Fabricate 2014*, UCL Press, London 2014.

[58] Fabio Gramazio, Matthias Kohler and Jan Willmann, *The Robotic Touch: How Robots Change*

Architecture, Park Books, Zürich 2014.

[59] Adam Greenfield, *Radical Technologies: The Design of Everyday Life*, Verso Books, London and New York 2017.

[60] Walter Gropius, *Scope of Total Architecture*, Harper & Brothers, New York and Evanston 1955.

[61] Walter Gropius, *Apollo in the Democracy. The Cultural Obligation of the Architect*, McGraw-Hill, New York 1967.

[62] Byung-Chul Han, *The Transparency Society*, Stanford University Press, Stanford 2015.

[63] Byung-Chul Han, *Psychopolitics: Neoliberalism and New Technologies of Power*, Verso Books, London and New York 2017.

[64] John Hejduk, *Education of an Architect. The Irwin S. Chanin School of Architecture of the Cooper Union*, Rizzoli, New York 1989

[65] John Hejduk, *Education of an Architect: a point of view. The Cooper Union School of Art and Architecture. 1964-1971*, The Monicelli Press, New York 1999.

[66] Michael Hensel, Achim Menges and Michael Weinstock (Eds.), *Emergence: Morphogenetic Design Strategies*, AD «Architectural Design», May-June 2004, Profile 169.

[67] Michael Hensel, Achim Menges and Michael Weinstock (Eds.), *Techniques and Technologies in Morphogenetic Design*, AD «Architectural Design», March-April 2006, Profile 180.

[68] Christopher Hight and Chris Perry (Eds.), *Collective Intelligence in Design*, AD «Architectural Design», September-October 2006, Profile 183.

[69] Christopher Hight, *Architectural Principles in the Age of Cybernetics*, Routledge, New York and London 2008.

[70] Bill Hillier and Julienne Hanson, *The Social Logic of Space*, Cambridge University Press, London and New York 1984.

[71] Bill Hillier, *Space Is the Machine*, UCL Space Syntax, London 2004.

[72] Eric J. Hobsbawm, *Age of Extremes. The Short Twentieth Century 1914-1991*, Pantheon Books, New York 1994.

[73] John H. Holland, *Emergence. From Chaos to Order*, Oxford University Press, Oxford and New York 1998.

[74] Rob Howard, *Computing in Construction. Pioneers of the Future*, Butterworth-Heinemann, Oxford 1998.

[75] Laura Iloniemi (Ed.), *The Identity of the Architect. Culture and Communication*, AD «Architectural Design», November-December 2019, Profile 262.

[76] Mimi Ito, *Apprendere Digitale*, Maria Grazia Mattei (Ed.), Egea, Milano 2015.

[77] Lisa Iwamoto, *Digital Fabrication: Architectural and Material Techniques*, Princeton Architectural Press, New York 2009.

[78] Charles Jencks (Ed.), *New Science = New Architecture?* , AD «Architectural Design», September-October 1997, Profile 129.

[79] Philip Johnson and Mark Wigley, *Deconstructivist Architecture*, The Museum of Modern Art, New York 1988.

[80] Steven Johnson, *Emergence. The connected lives of ants, brains, cities, and software*, Scribner, New York 2001.

[81] Ulrich Knaack, Sharon Chung-Klatte and Reinhard Hasselbach, *Prefabricated Systems: Principles of Construction*, Walter de Gruyter, Basel 2012.

[82] Branko Kolarevic and Kevin Klinger, *Manufacturing Material Effects – Rethinking Design and Making in Architecture*, Routledge, London 2008.

[83] Rem Koolhaas, *Delirious New York. A Retroactive Manifesto for Manhattan*, Oxford University Press, New York 1978.

[84] Rem Koolhaas, *Junkspace*, Quodlibet, Macerata 2006.

[85] Thomas S. Kuhn, *The Structure of Scientific Evolution*, University of Chicago Press, Chicago and London 1962.

[86] Neil Leach (Ed.), *Digital Cities*, AD «Architectural Design», July-August 2009, Profile 200.

[87] Neil Leach and Philip F. Yuan (Eds.), *Scripting the Future*, Tongji University Press, Shanghai 2011.

[88] Neil Leach, Achim Menges and Philip F. Yuan (Eds.), *Robotic Futures*, Tongji University Press, Shanghai 2015.

[89] Neil Leach and Roland Snooks (Eds.), *Swarm Intelligence: Architecture of Multi-Agent Systems*, Tongji University Press, Shanghai 2017.

[90] Neil Leach, Achim Menges and Philip F. Yuan (Eds.), *Digital Fabrication*, Tongji University Press: Shanghai, 2017.

[91] Lawrence Lessig, *La Trasparenza della Rete*, Maria Grazia Mattei (Ed.), Egea, Milano 2013.

[92] Pierre Lévy, *Cyberculture. Rapport au Conseil de l'Europe*, Edition Odile Jacob, Paris 1997.

[93] Pierre Lévy, *Collective Intelligence. Mankind's Emerging World in Cyberspace*, Perseus Books, New York 1997.

[94] Bruce Lindsey, *Digital Gehry. Material Resistance Digital Construction*, Birkhäuser, Basel 2011.

[95] Edward Lorenz, *The Essence of Chaos*, University of Washington Press, Washington 1993.

[96] Gabriella Lo Ricco and Silvia Micheli, *Lo Spettacolo dell'Architettura. Profilo dell'Archistar*, Bruno Mondadori, Milano 2003.

[97] Chris Luebkeman (Ed.), *2050. Designing Our Tomorrow*, AD «Architectural Design», July-August 2015, Profile 236.

[98] Greg Lynn (Ed.), *Folding in Architecture*, AD «Architectural Design», July-August 1993, Profile 102.

[99] Greg Lynn, *Animate Form*, Princeton Architectural Press, New York 1999.

[100] Benoit B. Mandelbrot, *The Fractal Geometry of Nature*, W. H. Freeman and Company, New York 1982.

[101] Humberto R. Maturana and Francisco J. Varela, *Autopoiesis and Cognition. The Realization of the Living* (1972), D. Reidel Publishing Company, Boston and London 1980.

[102] Wes McGee and Monica Ponce de Leon (Eds.), *Robotic Fabrication in Architecture, Art and Design 2014*, Springer, 2014.

[103] Marshall McLuhan, *Understanding Media. The Extensions of Man*, McGraw-Hill Book Company, New York 1964.

[104] Marshall McLuhan and Quentin Fiore, *The Medium is the Message. An Inventory of Effects*, Bantam Books, New York 1967.

[105] Achim Menges and Sean Ahlquist, *Computational Design Thinking*, AD Reader, Wiley, London 2011.

[106] Achim Menges (Ed.), *Material Computation*, AD «Architectural Design», March-April 2012, Profile 216.

[107] Achim Menges (Ed.), *Material Synthesis. Fusing the Physical and the Computational*, AD «Architectural Design», September-October 2015, Profile 237.

[108] Achim Menges, Tobias Schwinn and Oliver David Krieg, *Advancing Wood Architecture: A Computational Approach*, Routledge, London 2016.

[109] Achim Menges, Bob Sheil, Ruairi Glynn and Marilena Skavara, (Eds.), *Fabricate 2017*, UCL Press, London 2017.

[110] Fabio Merlini, *L'Estetica Triste. Seduzione e Ipocrisia dell'Innovazione*, Bollati Boringhieri, Torino 2019.

[111] Frédéric Migayrou with Zeynep Mennan (Eds.), *Architectures Non Standard*, Éditions du Centre Pompidou, Paris 2003.

[112] Melanie Mitchell, *An Introduction to Genetic Algorithms*, The MIT Press, Cambridge MA and London 1998.

[113] William Mitchell, *The City of Bits: Space, Place and the Infobahn*, The MIT Press, Cambridge MA and London 1995.

[114] Geoff Mulgan, *Social Innovation*, Maria Grazia Mattei (Ed.), Egea, Milano 2014.

[115] Nicholas Negroponte, *The Architecture Machine. Toward a More Human Environment*, The MIT Press, Cambridge MA and London 1970.

[116] Nicholas Negroponte, *Soft Architecture Machines*, The MIT Press, Cambridge MA and London 1975

[117] Nicholas Negroponte, *Being Digital*, Alfred A. Knopf, New York 1995.

[118] Kate Nesbitt, *Theorizing a New Agenda for Architecture. An Anthology of Architectural Theory 1965-1995*, Princeton Architectural Press, New York 1996.

[119] Samir Okasha, *Philosophy of Science. A Very Short Introduction*, Oxford University Press, Oxford and New York 2002.

[120] Kas Oosterhuis, *Hyper Bodies. Towards an*

E-motive Architecture, Birkhäuser, Basel 2003.

[121] Maria Luisa Palumbo, *New Wombs. Electronic Bodies and Architectural Disorders*, Birkhäuser, Basel 2000.

[122] Christiane Paul, *Digital Art*, Thames & Hudson, London 2003.

[123] Martin Pearce and Neil Spiller (Eds.), *Architects in Cyberspace*, AD «Architectural Design», March 1995, Profile 118.

[124] Stephen Perrella (Ed.), *Hypersurface Architecture*, AD «Architectural Design», May-June 1998, Profile 133.

[125] Brady Peters and Xavier De Kestelier (Ed.), *Computational Works. The Building of Algorithmic Thought*, AD «Architectural Design», March-April 2013, Profile 222.

[126] Brady Peters and Terry Peters, *Smart Geometry. Expanding the Architectural Possibilities of Computational Design*, AD Smart 01, Wiley, London 2013.

[127] Brady Peters and Terri Peters, *Computing the Environment. Digital Design Tools for Simulation and Visualisation of Sustainable Architecture*, AD Smart 06, Wiley, London 2018.

[128] Antoine Picon, *Digital Culture in Architecture. An Introduction for the Design Professions*, Birkhäuser, Basel 2010.

[129] Karl R. Popper, *Objective Knowledge. An Evolutionary Approach*, Oxford University Press, London 1972.

[130] Edy Portmann, Marco E. Tabacchi, Rudolf Seising, Astrid Habenstein (Eds.), *Designing Cognitive Cities*, Springer, 2019.

[131] Przemyslaw Prusinkiewicz and Aristid Lindenmayer, *The Algorithmic Beauty of Plants*, Springer-Verlag, New York 1990.

[132] Carlo Ratti, *Smart City, Smart Citizen*, Maria Grazie Mattei (Ed.), Egea, Milano 2014

[133] Carlo Ratti with Matthew Claudel, *Open Source Architecture*, Thames & Hudson, London 2015.

[134] Dagmar Reinhardt, Rob Saunders and Jane Burry (Eds.), *Robotic Fabrication in Architecture, Art and Design 2016*, Springer, 2016.

[135] Andreas Renz and Manuel Zafra Solas, *Shaping the Future of Construction. A Breakthrough in Mindset and Technology*, Technical Report, World Economic Forum, 2016.

[136] Gilles Retsin (Ed.), *Discrete. Reappraising the Digital in Architecture*, AD «Architectural Design», March-April 2019, Profile 258.

[137] Jeremy Rifkin, *La Terza Rivoluzione Industriale. Come il «Potere Laterale» Sta Trasformando l'Energia, l'Economia e il Mondo*, Oscar Mondadori, Milano 2011.

[138] Ernesto N. Rogers, *Editoriali di Architettura*, Gabriella Lo Ricco and Mario Viganò (Eds.), Zandonai, Rovereto 2009.

[139] Bernard Rudofsky, *Architecture without Architects. A Short Introduction to Non-Pedigreed Architecture*, Museum of Modern Art, New York 1964.

[140] Bernard Rudofsky, *The Prodigious Builders*, Harcourt Brace Jovanovich, New York and London 1977.

[141] Livio Sacchi and Maurizio Unali (Eds.), *Architettura e Cultura Digitale*, Skira, Milano 2003.

[142] Patrik Schumacher, *Digital Hadid. Lanscapes in Motion*, Birkhäuser, Basel 2004.

[143] Patrik Schumacher (Ed.), *Parametricism 2.0. Rethinking Architecture's Agenda for the 21st Century*, AD «Architectural Design», March-April 2016, Profile 240.

[144] Klaus Schwab, *The Fourth Industrial Revolution*, The Fourth Industrial Revolution, 2016.

[145] Jeffrey Schnapp, *Digital Humanities*, Maria Grazia Mattei (Ed.), Egea, Milano 2015.

[146] Emanuele Severino, *Il Destino della Tecnica*, BUR Rizzoli, Milano 1988.

[147] Emanuele Severino, *Tecnica e Architettura*, Raffaello Cortina Editore, Milano 2003.

[148] Bob Sheil, Mette Ramsgaard Thomsen, M., Martin Tamke and Sean Hanna (Eds.), *Design Transactions: Information Modelling for a New Material Age*, UCL Press, London 2020.

[149] Dennis Shelden (Ed.), *The Disruptors. Technology-Driven Architect-Entrepreneurs*, AD «Architectural Design», March-April 2020, Profile 264.

[150] Mike Silver (Ed.), *Programming Cultures: Art and Architecture in the Age of Software*, AD

«Architectural Design», July-August 2006, Profile 182.

[151] Andrea Sollazzo, *Digital Van Berkel. Diagrams Processes Models of UNStudio*, EdilStampa, Roma 2010.

[152] James Stevens and Ralph Nelson, *Digital Vernacular. Architectural Principles, Tools, and Processes*, Routledge, New York and London 2015.

[153] Mark Taylor (Ed.), *Surface Consciousness*, AD «Architectural Design», March-April 2003, Profile 162.

[154] Max Tegmark, *Life 3.0. Being Human in the Age of Artificial Intelligence*, Penguin Books, London and New York 2017.

[155] Kostas Terzidis, *Expressive Form*, Spon Press, London and New York 2003.

[156] Kostas Terzidis, *Algorithmic Architecture*, Elsevier Architectural Press, London and New York 2006.

[157] Skylar Tibbits (Ed.), *Autonomous Assembly. Designing for a New Era of Collective Construction*, AD «Architectural Design», July-August 2017, Profile 248.

[158] Alvin Toffler, *The Third Wave*, William Morrow, New York 1980.

[159] Ben Van Berkel and Caroline Bos, *Knowledge Matters*, Frame Publishers, Amsterdam 2016.

[160] Tom Verebes (Ed.), *Mass-Customised Cities*, AD «Architectural Design», November-December 2015, Profile 238.

[161] Anthony Vidler, *The Architectural Uncanny. Essays in the Modern Unhomely*, The MIT Press, Cambridge MA and London 1992.

[162] Paul Virilio, *The Informatic Bomb*, Verso, London and New York 1999.

[163] Paul Virilio, *City of Panic*, Berg Publishers, Oxford 2004.

[164] John Von Neumann, *The Computer and the Brain*, Yale University Press, New Haven and London 1958.

[165] Norbert Wiener, *Cybernetics or Control and Communication in the Animal and the Machine*, The MIT Press, Cambridge MA 1948.

[166] Jan Willmann, Fabio Gramazio, Matthias Kohler and Silke Langenberg, *Digital Materiality in Architecture*, Lars Müller Publishers, Baden 2008.

[167] Jan Willmann, Philippe Block, Marco Hutter, Kendra Byrne and Tim Schork (Eds.), *Robotic Fabrication in Architecture, Art and Design 2018*, Springer, 2018.

[168] Stephen Wolfram, *A New Kind of Science*, Wolfram Media 2002.

[169] Philip F. Yuan, *From Diagrammatic Thinking to Digital Fabrication*, Tongji University Press, Shanghai 2016.

Adknowledgements

This book would not have been possible without the support and input of many.

I am grateful to Pilar Maria Guerrieri for her daily support and for being one of the most important people in my life; to Domenica Bona for the fantastic job done for the graphics of this publication; to Tommaso Brighenti, a dear friend of endless conversations spent in talking about architecture as a labour of love and passion.

I am appreciative of all the support received by students, colleagues and professors at The Bartlett School of Architecture, UCL. Inside the school, I have learnt the real meaning of digital architecture in all its strengths and weaknesses, starting my studies from a humanistic point of view and finishing them with a much stronger technical awareness. I cannot recall the entire amount of things that I have learnt, but I certainly remember the most important one: for one thing that you learn, there are hundreds more to be discovered.

I would like to thank all the friends from my hometown, and all those friends and colleagues in the United Kingdom and spread around the world that I have had the pleasure to meet during almost ten years spent working and exploring different countries and cultures. Your endless patience in listening to my weird ideas is something that I cannot forget.

Thank you to my family for the endless support and for being the strong foundation upon which my life is built. You always give me the love and strength that I need. You are the solid roots from which my works and ideas start and grow.

My sincere apologies to those ones that I have certainly missed. I promise you will be at the top in my next work.

Last but not least, thank you to Architecture from an incompetent enthusiast.

About the author

Giuseppe Bono

RIBA Chartered Architect - ARB Registered Architect - Dott. Architetto, Ordine Architetti P.P.C. Milano

Giuseppe Bono is an Italian and British registered architect and senior postgraduate teaching assistant at The Bartlett School of Architecture, UCL. He holds a MArch(Hons) in Architecture and Construction Engineering from Politecnico di Milano, and he is now an MSc candidate in Architectural Computation at The Bartlett School of Architecture, UCL. With several years of international experience in the construction industry from conceptual design to built realisations, he combines professional work with academic research. He has worked in different countries around the world for a number of important clients and consultants, and has contributed to several lectures and international conferences at a number of important universities.